WILDBLUE PRESS
TRUE CRIME
features

JOHN FERAK
BODY OF PROOF
TAINTED EVIDENCE IN THE
MURDER OF JESSICA O'GRADY?

WILDBLUE
PRESS

WildBluePress.com

BODY OF PROOF published by:
WILDBLUE PRESS
1153 Bergen Pkwy Ste I #114
Evergreen, Colorado 80439

WILDBLUE PRESS is registered at the U.S. Patent and
Trademark Offices.

978-1-942266-21-1   *Mass Market Paperback ISBN*
978-1-942266-20-4   *eBook ISBN*

Interior Formatting/Book Cover Design by Elijah Toten
www.totencreative.com

Art Director Carla Torrisi Jackson

Editor Tom Panholzer
http://tpanholzer.wix.com/tom-panholzer

Contents

John Ferak

ACKNOWLEDGMENTS

This book chronicling the tragic murder of University of Nebraska at Omaha student Jessica O'Grady would not be possible without giving credit to so many people who helped directly or indirectly in the production of this story.

To my publishers at WildBlue Press, Steve Jackson and Michael Cordova, highly successful authors and the co-founders of WildBlue Press; Thomas Panholzer, editor; Carla Torrisi Jackson, art director; Elijah Toten, cover designer, formatter; Mackenzie Jackson, communications director; and Lauri Ver Schure of Murder by the Book in Denver, Colorado.

A number of reporters covered this case over many years at the *Omaha World-Herald*; the *UNO Gateway*, which is the University of Nebraska at Omaha student newspaper; The Associated Press; Omaha television stations KETV, KPTM, WOWT, KMTV; Nebraska Education Television (NET); and news radio station, 1110-AM KFAB. In particular, Bill Kelly of NET deserves special recognition for exemplary trial coverage. *Omaha World-Herald* reporters Todd Cooper, Christopher Burbach, and former reporter Lynn Safranek all provided outstanding news coverage chronicling the long trial. Omaha television reporters who also deserve recognition include Michelle Bandur, Brian Mastre, Kathy Niver, Carol Kloss, and others whose names I apologize for forgetting at this time.

I also owe a debt of gratitude to my wife, Andrea, a former newspaper copy editor, who helped edit the first draft of my book and always has great feedback and insight to share.

Most quotes in this book came from interviews I conducted with key people who had a direct or indirect tie to the Jessica O'Grady case, court transcripts, and public records that I reviewed. I am especially grateful to the timely help and exceptional assistance from the Douglas County Sheriff's Office, notably Sheriff Tim Dunning. I also want to single out Dave Kofoed, former Douglas County Sheriff's Office crime lab commander, for being gracious with his time and answering all of my questions. Those who also carved out time from their busy lives to answer my questions include Omaha lawyers James Martin Davis, Steve Lefler, Bill Gallup, and Clarence Mock; and international blood-stain expert Stuart James of Florida; criminal justice professor at the Peru State College Kelly Asmussen; retired Douglas County crime lab technician Darnel Kush; Lincoln Police Department forensics lab director Erin Sims; Lincoln criminal defense attorney Jerry Soucie; Omaha media personality Tom Becka; renowned national expert on no-body murder cases Tad DiBiase; founder of the Omaha chapter of the United States ATV Search and

Rescue Team D.J. Ginsberg; and former boyfriend of Jessica O'Grady Chayse Bates.

I also want to thank manager of Student Publications Josie Loza at *UNO Gateway*, the University of Nebraska at Omaha student newspaper. Josie dug through her student newspaper's archives to retrieve a number of vital photos that are being republished in this book. I also want to thank Douglas County District Court reporter Julie Hurley for her assistance in tracking down several court transcripts. As often as possible, I leaned upon court documents and other public records to recreate key dates and the sequence of events in this sad 2006 Nebraska murder case that remains a lively topic of conversation to this day.

A number of quotes in this book came from the various Nebraska media outlets referenced above. I also consulted with several articles written by the *UNO Gateway* and the *Omaha World-Herald*, including a few articles I wrote about this case during 2009 and 2012. As often as possible, I cited the respective news outlet that gathered the information. As part of my research in writing this book, I also had access to countless crime-scene photographs, hundreds of pages of court records, and Douglas County CSI forensic reports. Please be sure to read the Epilogue for this book. It's where I explain in great detail where my interest came in choosing to write this book in the manner that I've chosen. And it's also where you will read my direct challenge to Christopher Edwards.

John Ferak

BODY OF PROOF: TAINTED EVIDENCE IN THE MURDER OF JESSICA O'GRADY? is dedicated to three outstanding people who continue to have a major influence on my life, ambitions, and dreams.

To my parents, retired school teachers John and Cathy Ferak of Plainfield, Illinois. Thank you for setting a wonderful example. And to my only brother, Paul, a highly regarded lawyer in Chicago. I am eternally grateful for your talents and efforts to promote and market my book endeavors. Our friendship is strong and lasting.

"In battle, the United States Marine Corps is known as the tip of the spear. In a criminal investigation, akin to battle, the work of the first responders, detectives, and crime scene investigators is only the beginning of the process; however, their work is crucial to a successful outcome. The identification and arrest of a suspect is not the conclusion of the investigation, but the initiation of an equally vital chapter, the prosecution." – Dave Kofoed, *Forensic Investigation: From Crime Scene to Court Room*, a state of Nebraska law enforcement seminar, Aug. 21-22, 2008

Chapter 1

It was quite late, well past 11p.m., when Jessica O'Grady put the keys in her gray Hyundai Accent that she called "Francine" and drove off into the night from her apartment complex in Omaha, Nebraska.

The contents of her car depicted this dreamy college girl's life. She had an empty Mountain Dew bottle on the floor. Her college notebooks and a red-and-blue softball mitt were tossed on the seats.

Jessica, age 19, possessed a lot of redeeming qualities. She was cute, charismatic, and kind-hearted. Her wide-eyed charming smile and pretty hazel eyes made her a natural catch for guys. She stood about five foot nine. She had long, straight hair. Like a lot of teenage girls, Jessica was fond of tanning. She was a regular visitor to the Ashley Lynn tanning salon in Omaha.

Thanks to her fun-loving personality, Jessica had a lot of close friends. She giggled a lot. She also had a soft spot for animals. Her pet cat meant the world to her. Jessica always made sure Zoe had ample food and water.

Jessica helped coach one of her little niece's softball teams. The team of 7-year-olds was sure to smile whenever Jessica arrived at their practices and games. Jessica was their role model. She could do no wrong, and no wrong could be done to her.

Jessica chose to stay close to home after graduating from Omaha's Westside High School in 2004. From there, Jessica studied at the University of Nebraska at Omaha campus.

However, in the spring of 2006, she made up her mind not to return to the university for the coming fall semester of her third year. She was currently rethinking her college career plans and life's ambitions while she took that semester off. She had most recently majored in education.

Jessica worked part-time as a server at the Lone Star Steakhouse in west Omaha near the Oakview Mall. As she worked there, Jessica was starry-eyed. She longed for the right guy to sweep her off her feet, to wow her, to make her feel extra special.

When Jessica was a senior in high school at Westside, she held a part-time job as a register cashier at a Menards home improvement store in Omaha. Chayse Bates recalled how he was a cashier at the next closest register to Jessica. "We started chatting, and I just asked her out," Bates remembered years later. "We enjoyed going to movies. Jessica had one of the biggest and brightest smiles and was a very kind-hearted person."

During their romance, Jessica was fond of pop music, especially Top 40 music. She occasionally dragged Bates along to a chick-flick at the cinema, he said.

As time wore on, their relationship grew more serious.

"Jessica and I dated for about a year and a half," Bates said. "We even got an apartment together."

During the fall of 2005, shortly after Jessica's nineteenth birthday, however, their romance flamed out.

"We broke up because we wanted different things," Bates explained, "and we were too young to be living together. We cut ties completely after the break up. I never tried to contact her."

By 2006, Jessica, age 19, found herself living with a cute guy with short brown hair and brown eyes. He was six foot one, age 24, and weighed 190 pounds. If Jessica did not know much about Christopher McClanathan's past, the authorities did. McClanathan had been convicted back in 2001 of first-degree sexual assault in neighboring Sarpy County. After his release from incarceration, McClanathan was designated as a Level 3 convicted sex offender; the Nebraska State Patrol had classified him in the highest-risk category to reoffend. As he switched addresses, law enforcement alerted the local news media to publicize his new address.

Ultimately, Jessica broke off things with the convicted sex offender during the spring of 2006. Her friends were relieved. Their companionship was the perfect safety net if McClanathan grew jealous or angry toward her.

Not long after the break-up, a male coworker at the Lone Star Steakhouse caught her starry eye. She just couldn't stop thinking about him.

Coincidently, his name was also Chris. His full name was Christopher Edwards. They were both the same age. And, Jessica had visions of a long-term serious relationship with Edwards. He had graduated in 2005 from Burke High School on the city's west side. Edwards had brown hair, dark bushy eyebrows, and a pale skin tone. He was short and scrawny. He barely weighed 130 to 135 pounds. His clothes came from trendy retail stores such as Gap, America Eagle, and Hollister. He played lots of golf and kept a tennis racquet in his backseat.

At the steakhouse, Edwards tended the bar and waited on tables. It was not uncommon for him to work sixty hours a week. Here, Edwards was chatty, witty, and quite the tom cat. Naturally, Edwards had an ulterior motive for working nonstop at the Lone Star – his knocked up teenage girlfriend, Michelle Wilken, who also worked at the restaurant.

Subsequent court testimony later revealed that Wilken and Edwards began hooking up for sexual encounters around December of 2005.

Because Edwards was not bringing along condoms

13

for protection, Michelle's unplanned pregnancy the following month became inevitable. The pair of teenagers were forced to grow up real fast. Thinking he was obviously the father of Michelle's unborn child, Edwards agreed they would be mutually exclusive. He dropped out of college after attending classes during the fall semester at the nearby University of Nebraska at Omaha campus. By quitting college, Edwards picked up a lot more hours at the Lone Star, where he was in good graces with the management. He began to show aspirations of sliding into a management position himself. The wily Edwards said all the right things to please Michelle. In turn, she presumed he was a one-girl-kind-of-guy. She used the pregnancy like a giant magnet. She pulled Edwards closer to her, just like she wanted things to be.

Michelle liked to cuddle with Edwards in her arms. When she slept with him, she viewed him as her knight. She was proud to carry his future daughter in her womb.

It later became quite clear Edwards had other intentions. He was not ready to be tied down to only one girl.

Rather, he dared to engage in the dangerous and risky pursuit of other sexual exploits behind his pregnant girlfriend's back. Edwards's lustful eyes were on the prowl.

Sure enough, one pretty maiden, who also worked at the Lone Star Restaurant, caught his eye. She was quite tempting and desirous toward him: Jessica O'Grady. However, when it came to dating, Jessica had not always exhibited the best of judgment.

She was vulnerable to ill-fated choices.

Despite already knowing Edwards had a steady romance, Jessica was dazzled by the baby-faced, brown-haired bartender. She continued to make flirtatious overtures toward her coworker. She made sure Edwards knew in no uncertain terms she was available.

Edwards guessed his female coworker might be easy to sleep with. He was all about getting laid, and Jessica was carefree and adventurous.

Of course, Edwards had one giant obstacle in the way: his pregnant girlfriend, Michelle. She was still in high school and an aspiring beautician. But for Edwards, whose hormones were always raging, the temptation to engage in sexual escapades with Jessica could not be passed up.

Given the situation, it would seem Edwards was forced to make a tough choice. He could stick with his pregnant girlfriend or dump her for the flirty college girl at work who had a twinkle in her eyes.

But greed took over. Edwards wanted both. He was willing to play Russian roulette and engage in sexual conquests with both of these attractive women. But when it came to Jessica, there was no love. He just wanted her for her body, so he developed a game plan.He had to keep Michelle in the total dark about

Jessica. Michelle still lived at home with her parents, and since she lived under their roof, she had to abide by a strict 11 p.m. weekday curfew. It was mainly on the weekends when she and Edwards slept together, usually at his place on Saturdays. But Michelle could not track his constant whereabouts, especially during weekdays when they were not sleeping together under the soft sheets of his bed.

That April, Michelle wrongly assumed her boyfriend was being faithful to her and staying home alone as he should have been.

In reality, Jessica O'Grady had invited him over to her Omaha apartment complex. This was where she had settled after breaking off things with her most recent live-in boyfriend, Christopher McClanathan, the registered Level 3 sex offender. At her apartment, she proudly introduced Edwards to her friendly and accepting female roommates. These roommates didn't raise any major fuss to Edwards's presence at their apartment. And why would they? After all, Christopher and Jessica were flirty as they shared the couch together.

They giggled and laughed. Jessica was happy. Once, she pulled out an old photo album and showed Edwards pictures of herself as a child.

She was falling head over heels for this Edwards character. During their flings, Jessica blocked out the fact that Edwards already had another serious romance. Jessica had a rose-colored view of the world, and she longed to win Edwards over, hopefully sooner than later.

* * *

On one memorable night late that April, Jessica's female roommates retreated to their respective bedrooms, leaving her and Edwards alone in the living room. The roommates, snug in their beds, drifted off to sleep. As the night wore on, Jessica and Edwards retreated into Jessica's bedroom. There, they enjoyed each other's companionship underneath the covers.

After the sun came up the next morning, Jessica's roommates awoke first. They stumbled across some of Edwards's clothes strewn across the living room. The roommates also found his shoes placed on the outside of Jessica's still-shut bedroom door. The roommates knew what was up. It did not take much of a wild imagination to figure out what had taken place over night inside Jessica's apartment bedroom.

Later that day, Edwards rolled out of Jessica's bed. He scrounged up his clothes, dressed, and left her apartment building in his Honda Accord. Court testimony later showed Edwards was not entertaining thoughts about pursuing a long-term serious relationship with Jessica.

He viewed Jessica as nothing more than his secret sex partner. She was his extra booty call. His mind drifted back to his real girlfriend, Michelle. She was already about five months pregnant.

Naturally, he realized he needed to pacify Michelle, to make her feel special, his one and only—even if that was all a lie. He intended to keep Jessica on the periphery, at a safe distance.

But as the days wore on, Jessica emerged as a nagging problem.

She grew more passionate toward the Lone Star bartender even though he was two-timing his other more serious girlfriend to be with her. Jessica thoroughly enjoyed their time shacking up together, but she wished it to be more than that.

She wanted Edwards to be her Mr. Exclusive. She wanted his constant companionship and affection. She dreamed of a relationship that was bound to last, one that wasn't just based on passionate sex.

During the early part of May 2006, Jessica sought to win over her lover's heart. If she played her cards right, perhaps, Edwards might ditch Michelle, once and for all.

Christopher Edwards of Omaha worked as a waiter and a bartender at the Lone Star Steakhouse. Photo courtesy of The Gateway, University of Nebraska at Omaha's student newspaper.

Jessica O'Grady, 19, was a friendly and easy-going
sophomore at the University of Nebraska at Omaha campus.

Chapter 2

After a few short weeks involved in a dangerous love triangle with Christopher Edwards, Jessica O'Grady was anxious to deliver the news that no teenage boy with one already-pregnant girlfriend wants to hear:

"Guess what? I'm pregnant!"

Edwards quivered. The information left him jolted and taken aback. He didn't dispute the assertion. At first, he just took the news in stride. He stewed.

What Edwards might not have known was that Jessica had still been sexually active with Christopher McClanathan, her former boyfriend, just prior to her fling with Edwards. If she were indeed pregnant, there was a strong possibility Edwards might not be the biological father, after all.

Court testimony later made it clear that Jessica was not devastated by the prospect of being pregnant. Based on her line of thinking, she hoped her claim of being pregnant would convince Edwards to break things off with Michelle. That way, Edwards and Jessica could be an item, perhaps soul mates.

But Jessica could not have been more wrong.

Edwards had no time for shame and denial. He also did not act rationally. He figured he was in a real sticky mess. His careless and reckless sexual behavior in the bedroom was coming back to haunt him. His life was being turned upside down. Edwards realized he had two pretty girls fighting over his manhood, and both were pregnant. It was too late for second-guessing or rewinding the clock-of-life. Edwards now knew his ill-fated, poor lifestyle decisions of not using condoms during his risky sexual encounters had backfired on him a second time.

But what was Edwards to do about anything now? Surely, he would not dare to go back to Michelle and break this unflattering news to her. On the other hand, Edwards couldn't fathom the idea of being a father to different babies from different girlfriends at the same time.

He contemplated his next move.

Jessica was nice for casual sex, he rationalized, but she was never a serious girlfriend. In his mind, she was not marriage material, but Jessica's insistence of a pregnancy got to his head. He believed he had a real problem on his hands. He knew a pregnancy was not something he could just wish away from happening.

The mere hint of a pregnancy made him act quite uncomfortable. He underwent a sudden personality change. He started to act cold and cruel toward Jessica. He gave her the cold shoulder. He did not desire her presence any longer.

But Jessica knew what she wanted. And she wanted Chris Edwards. And if she was really pregnant this time around, she was optimistic about her future—a future that included a baby and Edwards.

Edwards's head spun like a Tilt-A-Whirl at the carnival. With each passing day, he grew more stressed about his disastrous predicament. So far, he had kept Michelle in total darkness about his sexual exploits with Jessica, including the alleged pregnancy. But sooner or later, Michelle would find out. After all, Jessica was blabbing to her friends, suggesting she was carrying Edwards's offspring.

What Edwards may not have known at the time was that at least one trusted confident of Jessica, the mother of one of her close friends, theorized that Chris McClanathan, not Christopher Edwards, was probably the father of Jessica's unborn child, if Jessica was indeed pregnant, court documents later noted.

But if Jessica were pregnant out of wedlock, she was set on whom she wanted to be the father. She wanted Edwards, not her old flame.

The weight of the world rested on Edwards's shoulders, and he was about to collapse. He was not even twenty years old, and yet he had two possessive lovers who were both pregnant. This was not the life he envisioned for himself.

He cared about Michelle. They were steady. But Jessica was a different story. The notion he had also gotten her pregnant gnawed at Edwards like an open bed sore. He was nervous. He was upset. And he did not have anybody to talk to about the mess.

In the solemn confines of his basement bedroom, Edwards sat in front of his laptop computer. Using the Google search engine, he typed the word "arteries." The website he opened included a diagram of the human body, subsequent court testimony would later reveal.

Carefully, Edwards studied the image. Indeed, the Google search would come in handy in the not too distant future.

* * *

The next day was Wednesday, May 10.

Edwards's mind was frazzled as he joined two long-time buddies for a round of golf. Only a couple of days earlier, he and Michelle had a serious heart-to-heart conversation, according to court testimony. Their conversation had nothing to do with Jessica. Edwards was still keeping his romance with her a deep, dark secret. Instead, when he and Michelle got together their conversation focused on the notion of wedding bells, according to court testimony. No plans were made, but their one-on-one talk was a clear signal of what Edwards envisioned for his future.

Still, Edwards knew he was not in a position where

he could just go out and buy an engagement ring for Michelle. After all, Jessica was still very much a part of the picture, and she very badly also wanted a long-term relationship. Edwards was in quite a fix. Out on the golf course, he remained uneasy, edgy, and tense. Edwards openly confided to one of his closest friends, Riley Wasserburger, how "he made a mistake. He got a girl pregnant," Wasserburger would later testify.

Edwards didn't mention the young lady's name, not that it mattered.

After the sun went down, Edwards and his friends eventually ventured over to a nearby cinema. A new horror film was playing, *An American Haunting*, starring Donald Sutherland and Sissy Spacek. When the movie let out, the sky was dark and the stars were out. The friends urged Edwards to join them for a late-night round of cards, but Edwards nixed the idea of playing poker.

He had other intentions. Everyone left the Omaha movie theater and headed their separate ways.

As for Edwards's not-so-discreet lover, Jessica, she had helped coach her niece's softball team earlier that evening. Afterward, she shared some intimate girl talk with her roommates while munching on pizza back at their apartment unit.

By now, Jessica had begun to embrace the idea of being pregnant, presuming she was indeed pregnant. She remained preoccupied with Edwards. She had peppered his cell phone with calls and text messages as he played golf and went to the movie theater with his boyhood pals that same evening.

Jessica was under the impression she had an open invitation to stop over and visit Edwards later that night. Back at her apartment, Jessica showered. She put on her make up. She changed into blue jeans, a pink T-shirt, and scooted her foot into a pair of flip flops. She was dolled up and attractive. Finally, she fetched her purse and cell phone and told her roommates goodbye, according to court testimony. Jessica also told them where she was going.

At approximately 11:15 p.m., Jessica exited her apartment building. In the parking lot, she climbed into her gray, four-door sedan and turned the ignition key.

It's about an eight-mile jaunt from Jessica's apartment complex in southwest Omaha over to the split-level brown, wood-frame home where Edwards resided in the Willow Wood subdivision. The route included lots of busy city intersections with signal lights.

Court records later made it clear that Jessica called one of her best friends at around 11:30 p.m. She told the friend, Kari Peterson, she was on her way to Edwards's place. About twenty minutes later, Jessica was nearing the dimly lit northwest Omaha subdivision where Edwards lived. His residence was in the vicinity of 132nd and Blondo Streets. Jessica grabbed her cell phone again, this time she dialed up Edwards. Eventually, she reached her destination.

Acting as the gracious host, Edwards let Jessica into the home through the garage and led her downstairs.

This was his Aunt Jane's house. She was in her late forties and worked for the Internal Revenue Service. She occupied the house with her daughter who was about fourteen years old at the time. Christopher Edwards lived in a downstairs living room that was converted into a spare bedroom in the secluded basement.

Among his interests, Edwards was a movie buff. His basement had a book shelf where he stored dozens of his favorite movies, including *Bourne Identity*, *Pirates of the Caribbean*, *Beverly Hills Ninja*, *Last Samurai*, *Resident Evil*, and *Gladiator*. He also owned a Denis Leary flick and a box collection of *The Best of Seinfeld*. Overall, the adjacent book shelves were mostly barren.

Over the next hour, things were probably uneventful as Edwards and Jessica spent time together. Jessica remained in her usual cheery, carefree demeanor. At approximately 12:20 a.m., she fired off a text message to her friend Kari.

"No shenanigans for Jessica," Jessica wrote.

She and Kari had come up with their share of code phrases. This one signified that Jessica was not planning to indulge in any sexual exploits that evening with Edwards, court testimony later showed.

In the best-case scenario, Jessica drifted off into a dreamy peaceful sleep on Edwards's comfortable bed, perhaps before 1 a.m.

* * *

After sunrise, Jessica's female roommates realized she had not returned home from the night before. Maybe Jessica simply made a last-minute decision to spend the night cuddling in her lover's arms. But as the day wore on, there was still no word from Jessica. Throughout the day, the baffled roommates flooded her cell phone with a ton of calls. They sent her a barrage of texts. Their calls went to voice mail. Their text messages all went unanswered.

Where was Jessica? Why was she ignoring her friends?

By evening, nothing changed. Her friends began to grow unglued. Her absence was perplexing. Something seemed wrong. Why had Jessica not called? Why had she not returned to her apartment?

Above all, her roommates knew it was totally out of character for Jessica to abandon her loving cat. And yet Jessica had gone an entire day without checking up on Zoe. Jessica was never the type to go bumming around without taking steps to ensure her favorite feline had food and water. Things were amiss.

That very same day, on May 11, Edwards drove over to the Walgreens store on North 132nd Street, a short distance from his home. A surveillance camera captured him inside the store at precisely 7:41 p.m. At the checkout counter, he bought white shoe polish, poster board paint, and correction fluid. He handed the cashier a ten dollar bill. She gave him back ninety-four cents.

After Edwards returned home, he shuffled down

the short flight of carpeted stairs. He applied gentle brush strokes across a section of ceiling above his bed. Next, he devoted his attention to his bedroom walls.

Some blankets, bed sheets, and pillows were yanked from the bed. Edwards flipped his mattress upside down. Two towels, one green and another blue, were later tossed into a black garbage bag that was put in the garage.

Thanks to a couple of plug-in air fresheners and some honey-melon-scented candles, the bedroom projected a friendly, inviting aroma. Edwards desired to make his bedroom appear as normal as possible. After all, he had another female guest arriving that weekend, his other pregnant girlfriend, Michelle.

* * *

In a different part of Omaha, Jessica's friends and family were not sleeping well at all. Their nights were restless and uneasy.

Their patience had worn thin. Their frustration mounted. They were grief-stricken, fearful, and distressed. Jessica had never been gone this long. They were in all-out panic mode.

Jessica was not reachable, but they didn't know why. Was she incapacitated? Had she crashed her car and rolled it down an embankment or steep ravine? Had her car broken down? And if so, had she encountered a dangerous stranger on her way back from Edwards's home? Was Edwards the culprit of her baffling disappearance?

Weekends at the Lone Star restaurant were typically busy. Jessica was on the schedule to work that Friday night. She failed to show.

The idea Jessica skipped town could not be completely discounted, but it seemed very, very unlikely to everyone who knew her. Nobody imagined Jessica chose to run off and not tell anybody. Foremost, why would Jessica leave without packing a suitcase? Why would Jessica abandon Zoe without giving her roommates instructions on feeding the cat?

Her family and friends sensed grave danger. They hoped it wasn't so.

Metropolitan Omaha has a sprawling population of about one million, and yet one nineteen-year-old University of Nebraska student seemed to have vanished into thin air.

If Jessica was endangered, her friends and family had to act fast to find her.

A day after Jessica O'Grady turned up missing Christopher Edwards frequented an Omaha Walgreens store on North 132nd Street to buy white-colored poster-board paint.

MISSING

http://iamssomething.com

Jessica O'Grady

AGE - 19
EYES - Hazel
HAIR - Brown
HEIGHT - 5' 9"
WEIGHT - 135
LAST SEEN -
May 10th, 2006
OMAHA,
NEBRASKA

Jessica O'Grady made a call from her cell phone just before midnight Wednesday May 10th, 2006 saying she was headed to the 120th and Blondo streets area. She has not been seen since.

Douglas County Sheriff
402-333-1000
PLEASE HELP

http://iamssomething.com

Friends and family of Jessica disseminated hundreds of flyers throughout Omaha in the hopes of finding someone who remembered seeing her after her late night disappearance on May 10, 2006.

Chapter 3

By the weekend, there was still no sign of the pretty college coed in Omaha.

Relatives had already gone ahead and contacted the Omaha Police Department to file a formal missing person's report. Missing person fliers began sprouting up across the city. Omaha's television stations were also notified about Jessica's disappearance. Photos of Jessica were plastered on the television screens in the hopes of jarring someone's memory.

The previous November, the Omaha Police Department took a nonchalant approach after being notified that a twelve-year-old black girl, Amber Harris, had vanished without a trace after getting off her school bus. Initially, the police wrongly presumed Amber might be a runaway. It later became clear a dangerous and violent convicted sexual predator named Roy Ellis Jr. had harmed Amber. He had buried Amber's bones in a secluded wooded area of North Omaha's Hummel Park. In the aftermath of Ellis's arrest and eventual conviction, the police department endured its share of stinging criticism about its handling of Amber's original missing person's report.

Since Jessica's family had contacted the news media from the get-go, the Omaha Police Department could not act lethargically and dismissively. The police knew the press was shining a light on their work. One investigator who spoke with Jessica's relatives and friends determined her disappearance did not seem natural. "O'Grady, her car, and her purse are the only things missing," detective Eric Nordby stated. "The rest of O'Grady's property is at her residence."

And thanks to the television news media, residents of eastern Nebraska and western Iowa began learning some of the details of Jessica O'Grady's disappearance.

Residents learned Jessica stood five foot nine and weighed between 135 and 150 pounds.

Her friends held out a glimmer of hope that maybe somebody, somewhere, had encountered Jessica. Unfortunately, it was all for naught. Eyewitnesses to her disappearance did not step forward. With every passing hour, Jessica's family and friends lost a little more hope. Their worst fears began to creep into their minds. Perhaps Jessica was not coming home. Perhaps she was not alive.

"It's been extremely hard," Jessica's mother, Rachelle, "Shelly" told Omaha television KETV. "Every day, every hour that goes by, your heart just sinks even more."

Omaha's television stations gave Jessica's unfolding story a serious tone. The circumstances did not fit the profile of a typical teenage runaway. It did not take long before the Jessica O'Grady mystery captured the hearts of Omaha. The city sensed something was wrong. It was rare for someone, anyone, to turn up missing in Omaha, especially a college coed who had so much to live for.

***

Because Jessica might have been the victim of foul play, a number of area waterways and lakes were searched in hope of recovering Jessica's body.

Among those areas searched were Standing Bear Lake, nestled along 132nd Street in Northwest Omaha and Zorinsky Lake Park, a popular destination to picnic and for joggers to loop around in far West Omaha at 156th and F Streets. In the vicinity of State Highway 36, North-Central Omaha's spacious Cunningham Lake encompassed more than one thousand fifty acres. Besides boating, this massive scenic lake had areas for campers and horseback enthusiasts.

In addition to the lakes, the meandering Elkhorn River was believed to be another spot where Jessica's body might wash up. The Elkhorn flowed approximately two-hundred-ninety miles across Nebraska before it joined the Platte River on the edge of Omaha. There were plenty of mud bars and submerged logs, prime spots for a human body to become lodged.

Hundreds of kind-hearted and vigilant volunteers came together in unison. They waded across the marshy riverbanks. They trudged through mud and silt along the sandy shorelines of the Elkhorn River. They scoured thick and dense underbrush and shrubs. They poked around large rocks. They looked underneath large cottonwood and willow trees, all in a desperate attempt to find Jessica. Volunteers gave their all as they swatted away the biting mosquitoes and brushed away ticks and bugs. These were dedicated and caring souls. Many had never met Jessica but had been drawn to the call of duty after learning of her family's heart-wrenching ordeal through the Omaha news media.

Oddly enough, one young man in Omaha avoided the search party efforts like the plague. Yet he had been the last person to see Jessica alive.

Christopher Edwards intentionally chose to lay low. He did not want any notoriety. He did not want his name and face plastered across the television screens. Simply put, he avoided the search party efforts at all costs.

Instead, Edwards spent the weekend with Michelle, inviting her over to his home when he was not working. Michelle later gave an account that nothing in her boyfriend's basement bedroom appeared unusual or out of the ordinary. Most of all, she did not notice anything odd or terrorizing about her boyfriend's bed.

Just a few days after Jessica visited his place and never returned home, Edwards and Michelle frolicked under the cover of his bed sheets. By this point, Edwards knew that Jessica was not a threat to his relationship with Michelle any longer.

Of course, hiding out and pretending Jessica's disappearance was all a figment of everybody else's imagination had its dire and disastrous consequences.

Obviously, Jessica's friends all knew that Edwards was sexually intimate with Jessica. Her friends were also aware Jessica was on her way over to Edwards's house at the time she vanished.

One of Jessica's roommates even stopped by the Lone Star while he was working on Saturday to ask Edwards questions about Jessica's whereabouts, but he quickly dismissed her curiosity. Edwards was as icy and cold-blooded as a slithering snake and showed absolutely no interest in helping to find Jessica.

So far, Edwards's name had not yet surfaced in the news reports. He was not being identified as a possible suspect in her disappearance nor was the police breathing down his neck. He seemed to be in the clear. But how long would that last?

Chapter 4

Exuberant little girls arrived on time at the Omaha softball complex with their families and loved ones. The build up to the Sunday game was about the last glimmer of hope for Jessica's frantic friends and unnerved family.

Jessica would never skip a softball game. She loved to coach these young, caring, and enthusiastic grade-school girls.

Sadly, though, Jessica was a no-show that afternoon on the ball diamond. It was the latest of many dark and scary signs that pointed to the strong harsh dose of reality that something awful had already happened to Jessica.

That same weekend, dozens of customers casually went about their business inside the Lone Star restaurant. Adults sat at their respective booths. They sipped on sodas. Others drank domestic beers. They cut up juicy steaks and ate their buttered baked potatoes. They chatted about their lives, and some of them even probably talked about the missing person's case dominating Omaha's television airwaves that middle-of-May weekend.

One person who showed up that weekend did not drop by for a tasty meal or the ambiance. This woman had a look of intensity. Most of all, she was desperate for clear answers about her missing niece.

Shauna Stanzel came to the Lone Star because she knew Jessica's lover, Christopher Edwards, was probably working. Jessica and her aunt were very close. In fact, Jessica had lived with her aunt as a teenager. Jessica's mother had her when she was only fourteen years old. Fortunately, Jessica's aunt offered her a more stable home life. Jessica and her aunt gelled. Even after Jessica moved out and attended college, both women saw each other regularly. When Jessica turned up missing, her aunt took a leading role to find her.

That Sunday at the Lone Star, Edwards, a boyish-looking chap, was busy pouring drinks and chatting with his customers around near the bar. Until this moment, his efforts to fly under the radar were going according to plan. Now, suddenly, Edwards was a bit uneasy. Jessica's worried and upset aunt was in his face.

Edwards projected an evil vibe. He had a hollowed soul and acted dismissively. He brushed off Jessica's disappearance as no big deal. He didn't seem the least bit worried about her welfare or what might have happened to her.

That afternoon, he foolishly told an obvious lie that later came back to haunt him. He told the heartbroken aunt that Jessica never showed up at his home back on Wednesday night, May 10. Instead, he claimed he broke off plans for Jessica to stop over to his place that night. He implied he had not seen Jessica since Tuesday, May 9.

* * *

As Omaha's television stations spread the word about the missing coed, they included information about the make and model of Jessica's vanished car. The enormous publicity boost made a quick difference.

By Tuesday, May 16, an Omaha businessman spotted Jessica's missing 2001 Hyundai Accent, bearing Nebraska license plates PEI 894. Her abandoned car had been left in the parking lot of a shopping center, just across the street from the Lone Star.

Omaha Police Department detectives converged upon the scene. The car was locked. The keys were missing. The city police crime lab was called out. Technicians dusted the vehicle for fingerprints and later tested for possible DNA evidence. Police learned that Jessica's car had probably been left in the parking lot for at least three or four days. However, there was no evidence pointing to the possibility that Jessica drove there, parked, and then vanished into thin air.

In other words, someone else had gained access to Jessica's car and intentionally put it there.

Obviously, the startling discovery of Jessica's abandoned car widened Omaha's biggest crime mystery. Her car was barely a block from the Lone Star where she and Edwards worked. The recovery of Jessica's car became a key turning point in her missing person case. It upped the stakes. The Omaha Police Department now began to treat Jessica's case as a criminal probe.

The investigation also took on a stronger sense of urgency.

For the first time, a handful of Omaha police detectives raced out to the home of Jane Edwards on North 130th Street. The properties in the Willow Wood subdivision were mostly a collection of starter homes on small lots. The Edwards home was built in 1982 and valued at about $125,000, according to the Douglas County Assessor's Office. This residence had a double-wide concrete driveway and a concrete stoop that led to the front door entrance. Several shrubs lined the front of the house. A tall tree stood sentinel over the driveway. The vinyl frame multi-level home had brick veneer. Besides the three main bedrooms, the property had the extra spare bedroom where Edwards lived in the basement.

Edwards had moved into his aunt's house after finishing high school. His own parents had divorced years earlier. The opportunity to come and go out of his aunt's home was convenient. His bedroom in the basement gave him loads of personal privacy. His carpeted room measured about fifteen feet by fourteen feet. Photos of his room showed a bed, nightstand, a desk, and chair. He also had a television, stereo, and a couple of wooden bookcases. Police photos of his room show his bedroom closet in disarray. He kept several pricey, short-sleeved collared shirts on hangers in his closet. He also had a number of hockey jerseys and several pairs of expensive dress shoes.

* * *

When the team of Omaha Police detectives arrived at the Edwards residence, they did not know what to expect. But they figured that the teenager identified by the missing young woman's friends as being Jessica's boyfriend could hopefully fill in some huge gaps. Her mystifying disappearance had now stretched into its second week. Surely, Edwards was on high alert. He knew the risks of talking with the police. Yet, he erred on the side of showing a cooperative side. This may have been a ploy to throw off the detectives and hope they fell for his pathetic charade. Both he and his aunt who owned the home agreed to voluntarily let the police detectives inside the home.

Of course, Edwards failed to realize that once the police were let inside his aunt's home, the nosy detectives were sure to poke around, given his girlfriend's unexplained absence. These Omaha police detectives, Jim Arndt, Eric Nordby, and Sgt. Mark Desler, were not a bunch of Keystone cops. Rather, they were highly trained professionals who had a nose to sniff out suspicion, including foul play. Foremost, they were sharp enough to keep their emotions in check. They did not want Edwards to catch on or read into their suspicions. They knew there was a strong possibility Jessica came into harm's way during an encounter with Edwards, since he was her intimate sexual partner.

As far as Edwards was concerned, he must have thought he had no reason to sweat. During the casual conversation with police, Edwards claimed he was supposed to meet Jessica on the night of May 10, but then he called her and canceled plans.

At one point, the inquisitive detectives asked Edwards if he minded letting them look around his bedroom. Edwards reacted with a sign of hesitance.

"Like in a few days," he suggested.

With his aunt standing nearby, he turned to her and said, "I'd rather do it tomorrow," he begged.

Whether he realized it or not, Edwards had given the police a strong vibe. He did not want them poking around his bedroom for some reason. The police took this as a direct signal that Edwards wanted to buy more time to conceal or destroy damning evidence. The police moved to reassure Edwards that he was in charge of the event. The police tried to act like they were his friends. They would only look at locations in his room that were mutually agreed upon. "At any point, you don't want us to look in some area, we don't go in that area. You control this search," one detective explained.

Edwards relented. He obliged their request to get a sneak peek of his room.

Down in the bedroom, the moment grew intense. Finally, the detectives took a bead on the bed. Suddenly, Edwards spoke up. He expressed deep reluctance. He did not want the detectives poking around at the covers of his bed.

At that moment, the detectives could have backed off and gone upstairs and left. But the Omaha police detectives understood the stakes and the magnitude of the situation. Jessica was missing, probably slain. Her deceitful boyfriend stood at the foot of his bed. He appeared to be the mastermind of her disappearance. Clearly, Edwards was hiding something.

One of the detectives, Jim Arndt, thought fast.

He and Edwards had discussed the idea that perhaps Jessica had chosen to commit suicide. This was certainly not the case, but Arndt broached the subject strictly to win over the suspect's confidence and make Edwards feel at ease. Perhaps Jessica left behind a note, a suicide note, tucked underneath the mattress, the persistent detective offered.

Even though Edwards obviously did not want the police going near his bed, he caved in. He fell for the detective's ploy. He gave the police permission to lift up the blankets on his bed.

At that point, Edwards was sunk.

The Omaha police detectives saw blood, and a whole lot of it. Subsequent police photos of the bedroom showed the underside of Edwards's mattress to be drenched in human blood. Police reports indicated the blood was still moist and damp, even though Jessica had already been missing a week. The bloody mattress was gruesome, but police saw more blood rampant within the room.

Tiny flecks of blood spatter had turned up on Edwards's clock radio, his headboard, his nightstand, and the ceiling directly above the suspect's bed. When the police detectives inquired about the blood on the headboard, Edwards shrugged. He replied that he had recently cut his wrist.

Edwards realized he was in deep trouble. So he backpedaled. He claimed he had sexual intercourse with Jessica on his bed. During their sex, she was in the midst of her menstrual cycle, thus causing the blood loss, he claimed.

Naturally, the police did not buy his outrageous and preposterous story.

Suddenly, the mood turned adversarial. Edwards had put himself in a perilous situation. He no longer wanted the Omaha police hovering around his bedroom. The detectives decided they needed to obtain a formal search warrant to remain inside the home. The aunt's residence was now being classified as a crime scene based on the revelation of the bloody mattress.

However, Jessica's case was about to undergo a dramatic change surrounding the investigation. The Omaha Police Department was forced to bow out of the criminal case altogether, but not necessarily by choice.

Later that night, the Edwards probe was officially transferred over from the Omaha Police Department to the Douglas County Sheriff's Office. Someone discovered the Edwards home was technically outside City of Omaha limits. Therefore, the crime scene dictated the case be administered by the sheriff's office.

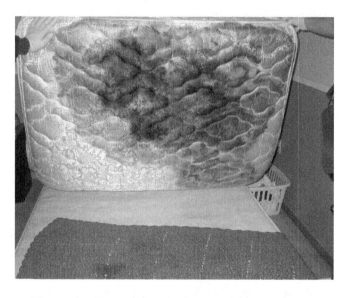

This is what detectives at the Omaha Police Department saw when they lifted up the mattress of Edwards during their search for his missing lover, Jessica O'Grady.

Chapter 5

The Douglas County Sheriff's Office wasted no time. Its crime lab swarmed in and took over the case from the Omaha Police Department, just hours after the bloody mattress was uncovered.

By midnight, a couple of the Douglas County crime lab personnel, Josh Connelly and Christine Gabig, rushed over to the unfolding crime scene in the Willow Wood subdivision. Douglas County CSI commander Dave Kofoed was quickly apprised of the disturbing situation.

Although Kofoed was hired to manage the crime lab, he preferred to get a piece of the action himself. He typically thrust himself into collecting clues and testing the evidence back at the crime, despite having employees who were hired to do such tasks. Kofoed had previously worked for a decade at the Omaha Police Department, where he served as a night-shift supervisor in its crime lab. Kofoed enjoyed the adrenaline rush and fast-paced nature of investigating violent crimes and murders. He became obsessed with acquiring clues to nail any hideous individual who committed murder. When Kofoed left Omaha to take over the Douglas County crime lab by 2000, his burning desire to remain a fixture at processing crime scenes never flamed out.

As Kofoed rolled up in his county-owned vehicle to the dreary Edwards multi-story home, the neighborhood buzzed with an unusual and uncomfortable police presence in the middle of the night. Christopher Edwards was also there since, so far, he had not been arrested in connection with any crime. With the police raid in high gear, Kofoed pulled aside a few Omaha police detectives still lingering around the home.

Kofoed spoke with Omaha Police Lt. Alex Hayes. Hayes was a sharp, serious, and no-nonsense homicide detective who would later serve as the Omaha Police chief from 2010 to 2012. Hayes and Kofoed had previously worked together.

Kofoed knew he was in for a long night. His CSI team would spend approximately ten hours inspecting the Edwards home.

"I remember that night as being a lot of tedious and methodical crime-scene work," Kofoed said. "I remember that I felt really lucky to have Josh (Connelly) and Christine (Gabig) at the scene."

That night, the pair had the task of processing the suspect. The event took place in the main-level living room. A clump of head hairs were taken from Edwards. Connelly took numerous photos of Edwards.

48

CSI Gabig processed the suspect for fingerprints and fingernail clippings. She also obtained the all-important buccal swab from Edwards's mouth. The swab would be stored at the Douglas County crime lab since it contained Edwards's precious DNA sample.

Connelly put his videography skills to the test, documenting the outside and inside of the multi-story home. All told, Gabig captured almost one hundred seventy-five photographs of the property. Many of her photos concentrated on the garage. She took numerous photos of the suspect's car and various objects within his bedroom.

Gabig made it a priority to focus upon the suspect's bedroom ceiling. She noted in her forensic reports that blood spatter was present in the area above Edwards's bed. "Numerous small spots were visible to the naked eye," Gabig stated.

The CSIs went ahead and used tape to grid sections of the ceiling. Inevitably, Luminol, a specialized fluorescent chemical used to detect invisible blood stains, was sprayed upon the ceiling, plus the basement walls. Reactions for blood were found on the ceiling, south wall, and west wall, Gabig stated.

Meanwhile, Kofoed was deciphering the case and getting a first-hand view of the bloody crime scene in the basement. However, he was not an impartial, neutral, or unbiased fact-finding CSI sleuth, as most people in the forensic profession tend to operate. In

49

fact, years later, trial testimony conclusively proved that the Douglas County CSI commander had a knack for manufacturing clues back at his crime lab.

By the time he arrived at the home of Edwards, Kofoed had already gotten away with planting blood in at least two different high-profile murder cases within Nebraska's Heartland. The head law enforcement official tasked with avenging Jessica's death was a criminal himself. He was a master evidence planter, manipulator, and con artist, who just had not been exposed as of 2006. The months and years ahead would prove to bring a most interesting chess match for Nebraska's court of law. Back at the time of Jessica's disappearance, others in Nebraska law enforcement were still oblivious to any possible scandals brewing. Kofoed had yet to be accused of being shady or corrupt.

As the first night of the CSI investigation wore on, it did not take long for Kofoed to realize the murder suspect was a ball of evil. Edwards was not a sympathetic figure in the eyes of the Omaha community at large. The Burke High School graduate had a darkened soul. Clearly in Kofoed's mind, Edwards had taken liberties to hide his lover's dead body to avoid being prosecuted for her killing. But Edwards made a giant and colossal error.

Wrongly, Edwards presumed that all the cops and CSIs conducting the criminal investigation would be on the up and up. He counted on them being honest and acting with the utmost of integrity. The murder suspect never fathomed that the key leader put in charge of supervising the CSI forensics investigation of Jessica's disappearance would later be proven to be shady, manipulative, and underhanded.

During his tenure, the CSI commander was often on the prowl, sniffing around for sensational murder cases to keep his Douglas County Sheriff's Office crime lab in the constant news media spotlight.

Murder was a giant chess game for Kofoed. He considered himself the winner every time he waltzed into a criminal courtroom and glared into the eyes of the guilty killer wearing the orange, jail-issued jumpsuit, leg shackles, and steel handcuffs. Whenever a case concluded, Kofoed was eager and ready for the prime-time Omaha television cameras to crowd around him. He loved to brag about the great work being performed by the crime lab he managed.

In contrast, the upper command staff at the Omaha Police Department during that period typically shunned the news media. The city police force often refused to be cooperative unless the press was inquiring about a murder case that was already solved and adjudicated in the court system. The civilian employees who toiled away as true public servants for the Omaha Police Department crime lab were nameless, faceless figures. Omaha's crime lab personnel were rarely, if ever, on television. Their identities were largely unknown to residents of the sprawling metropolitan city nestled along the Missouri River.

Quite the opposite was true at the Douglas County

crime lab, thanks to Kofoed's savvy marketing schemes. He was accustomed to the local press treating him like English royalty; while his former employer, the Omaha Police Department, was content to let its hard work and diligence in solving crimes speak for it.

From the outset, it seemed Jessica's case might prove challenging for the authorities in Omaha, but Kofoed's insatiable need for constant public gratification only fueled his motivation to get her case solved quickly. He immersed himself in the particulars of the crime. He was eager to get busy and build a treasure trove of evidence. For the sake and relief of the Omaha community, Edwards needed to be locked down for Jessica's apparent murder. After all, this was an unusually heartbreaking and tragic murder mystery.

Jessica never deserved to die so young. And her family deserved closure and the chance to heal. The despicable wild animal who savagely killed her needed to be punished for his horrible and unconscionable deeds. But what made this Omaha murder case so unusual was that a scorpion was investigating the serpent.

* * *

During his first night at the crime scene, the county crime lab commander did happen to produce a couple of noteworthy bloody clues as he poked around the Edwards home. Kofoed reported he retrieved a lime green bath towel and a teal blue towel as he dug through a black trash bag left in the enclosed garage.

Both towels appeared to be drenched with darkened blood stains.

In the aftermath of Jessica's slaughter, Edwards surely scrambled in his frenzied state of mind to wipe up the blood spatter rampant throughout his bedroom. Towels were intuitively thrown into a trash bag.

Unfortunately for Edwards, the garbage truck had not come soon enough. Rather, a host of Nebraska law enforcement officials had converged upon his house on Tuesday, May 16, and Edwards was ill-prepared for their arrival.

Besides the two bloody towels in the garage, some blankets and quilts near Edwards's bed were retrieved. This bedding also contained signs of blood spatter.

In retrospect, Edwards's laziness in disposing of the crucial evidence was not entirely unexpected. And Jessica's homicide would not be the first time a cunning and calculated premeditated killer, who thought he had covered his tracks so masterfully, had only fooled himself.

Kofoed's recovery of the two bloody towels solidified his self-confidence. It helped reaffirm his mindset that he was the absolute greatest CSI in America's Heartland.

However, the bloody towels paled in comparison with the successful discovery of the blood-soaked mattress by the trio of Omaha police detectives who managed to get into the house first.

Without a doubt, the bloody mattress was the most precious and sensational clue. But that was not a clue Kofoed could claim credit for finding. His comrades from the Omaha Police Department had identified the blood-soaked mattress without help or guidance from him.

The bedding was downright grotesque, shocking, and overly dramatic. If Jessica's case went to a jury trial, Kofoed might be poised to serve as one of the back-of-the-line witnesses for the prosecution. Sure, his recovery of two bloody towels was impressive and exhibited good forensics legwork, but nobody would care or really remember those details long after Jessica's murder case was over. It stood to reason that the Omaha Police Department could wind up as the heroes of the case for recovering the mattress and identifying Edwards as the prime suspect.

Luckily for Kofoed, one giant roadblock barrier was pleasantly taken away. The Omaha Police Department was out of the equation. The Edwards investigation was being handled by the Douglas County Sheriff's Office. Kofoed would retain and control the key physical evidence. The city police detectives would fade out of the case, though their contributions were monumental and lasting.

As fate would have it, the bloody mattress was indeed coming back to the Douglas County Sheriff's Office Property and Evidence Room. That room and the biohazard room were secure areas Kofoed managed and gave himself 24/7 access. At the sheriff's office, Kofoed did not have to worry about nosy detectives and overly ambitious CSI personnel constantly peering over his shoulder. He had the keys to the office. He was the lone supervisor in the CSI unit, which consisted of about a dozen full-time subordinates. All of the crime lab employees answered to him since he was their boss.

At the Douglas County CSI facility, Kofoed dictated all of his crime lab staff's assignments. He set their schedules. He determined when they came and when they left. As bizarre as it sounds, Kofoed was not adverse to sleeping overnight inside his commander's office or pulling a 24-hour shift.

When it came to oversight and accountability, Kofoed was not on a long leash—he was on no leash at all. After all, the sheriff and his top-level command staff knew little about forensics. They entrusted the management of the crime lab to Kofoed because they thought he was a skilled seasoned pro. In reality, a cunning, sly red fox guarded the henhouse.

For instance, even though the Douglas County crime lab was classified as a secure and restricted area, the facility in suburban northwest Omaha lacked security cameras or surveillance video. None of this bode well for any suspect linked to the Jessica O'Grady disappearance and murder.

* * *

After pulling an all-nighter at the Edwards home, Kofoed and his diligent CSIs loaded up their crime lab van the following morning well after sunrise. The property was given back to its rightful occupants. Even though authorities did not find Jessica's body anywhere on the property, the CSI unit had hauled away the bloody mattress. That act alone was a huge deal and a definite game-changer for the suspect. The river of blood measured more than eight feet in diameter across the mattress. Jessica's blood had seeped more than two inches deep. The blood soaked through the foam mattress and into the box springs underneath.

So much blood had saturated into the mattress that investigators became certain that Jessica was surely not among the living. Unfortunately, the frustrated investigators did not know where her body was taken. Edwards had had nearly a full week's lead time to dispose of her body.

As for Edwards, he wasn't talking anymore. Given the striking turn of events, Edwards and his family made the conscious decision to cease communications with the cops. They pretty much refused to cooperate with law enforcement investigators in the case from that moment forward.

For the time being anyway, Edwards remained free. But how long would his freedom last?

On the night of May 16, 2006, Omaha Police and the Douglas County Sheriff's Office CSI unit executed a search warrant at this home in connection with the apparent homicide of Jessica O'Grady.

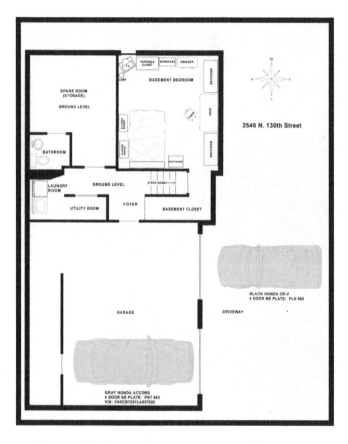

The Douglas County CSI unit constructed this diagram depicting the interior of the home belonging to Jane Edwards. Her nephew lived in her basement, where the blood-soaked mattress was found.

Chapter 6

Around Omaha, James Martin Davis was regarded as Nebraska's most media savvy criminal defense attorney.

One of Omaha's most affable personalities, Davis was Nebraska's version of the late Johnny Cochrane, the famous criminal defense lawyer who represented Brentwood murder defendant O.J. Simpson.

In Omaha, Davis never passed up a chance to take on a high-profile case destined for significant news media coverage and robust public discussion on the Nebraska talk radio shows. Rarely a week passed without Davis summoning a pack of journalists to his magnificent downtown Omaha law office on Farnam Street for a press conference. A short, stocky lawyer with salt and pepper hair, Davis was witty with a sharp legal mind. He was notorious for trying his client's criminal cases in front of the news media, much to the angst of the judges, fellow lawyers, and many prosecutors, who were not accustomed to working with a rare lawyer such as James Martin Davis.

Other attorneys and the judges might have despised his techniques of constantly courting the press, but Davis was an excellent trial lawyer, nonetheless, a force to be reckoned with.

Back in the 1960s, Davis was a combat soldier in the U.S. Army over in Vietnam. He later served in the U.S. Secret Service from 1970 to 1973. However, he became best known for his highly successful career as an Omaha defense attorney. Davis was a wise lawyer because he also knew when he had taken on a client who faced unwinnable odds.

On May 17, 2006, a matter of hours after the bloody mattress was confiscated, the nineteen-year-old murder suspect met with Davis. The meeting was arranged by the suspect's domineering father, Bob Edwards.

Davis recalled it was a frustrating and challenging case to take on because Bob Edwards wanted to be part of all of the discussions between Davis and his son. Complicating matters, Davis was hearing from law enforcement investigators that they suspected Chris Edwards had someone help clean his room, possibly removing blood spray from some of his basement walls.

On the other spectrum, Davis surmised that Jessica's family was desperate for answers. They wanted to recover her body, to give her a burial with dignity.

Davis began to contemplate a strategy for his new, teenage client. Even though Chris Edwards had not been charged with any crimes, Davis had a bad vibe about his client's dire predicament.

***

Around Omaha, Douglas County Sheriff Tim Dunning was a clever politician, who was dedicated to the mission and value of police work and keeping the community safe. Dunning maintained high standards for those who worked for him, and he was conscientious about solving cases that involved violent crime. The sheriff also mastered the art of manipulating the Omaha news media when it worked to his advantage. Dunning had retired from the Omaha Police Department after twenty-two years on the force. In 1994, he was elected as the sheriff of Nebraska's largest county, and from there he built up his political fiefdom and powerbase. Voters would reelect Dunning in 1998, 2002, 2006, 2010, and again in 2014. In most general elections, Dunning ran unopposed.

In 2006, as Omaha headed into another hot, sweltering summer, Dunning wanted everyone to realize that the city's biggest murder case was in capable hands. After all, Kofoed was in charge of the forensics work. Dunning also used the media to demonize his prime suspect. The sheriff knew that Edwards and his family were sure to keep a close eye on any activity surrounding Jessica's case in the television broadcasts, radio stations, and the newspaper.

Dunning wanted the suspect's family to perceive the walls closing in. Therefore, Edwards was portrayed as an outcast, a pariah, a parasite. His days as a free man were surely numbered, the sheriff assured the media.

"I think we're going to deal well with this particular case in a short amount of time," Dunning confidently told the Omaha newspaper. "I think there is a lot of good evidence for investigators to work on here."

Regardless of Sheriff Dunning's glowing optimism and wishful thinking, it was unclear whether an arrest was truly imminent.

The absence of a body meant no autopsy had been conducted. The absence of an autopsy report left law enforcement without an official cause and manner of death. Was Jessica stabbed? Beaten? Shot? Prosecutors would have no other option but to speculate and dish up their best guesses as to how their victim met her cruel and tragic death. Secondly, the CSI unit failed to turn up a possible murder weapon during its initial tedious inspection of rummaging through Edwards's home on the night his bloody mattress was seized.

Generally speaking, many criminal prosecutors across the country are reluctant to charge a defendant with murder when there is no confirmation the victim is deceased. In Jessica's case, there was no death certificate even on file at the City-County government building to confirm she died.

Indeed, there were a number of giant barriers standing in the way of a murder conviction against Edwards. But Kofoed was a relentless investigator. He was not intimidated by the daunting case ahead of his unit.

He knew he was up to the task.

And, if he played his cards right, Jessica's murder case might catapult him into the national CSI limelight. There might be crime shows, documentaries, and re-enactments of the Jessica O'Grady murder in households all over the country.

For the time being, however, this was just dreamy, wishful thinking. For great things to materialize, Kofoed needed to secure the arrest of Edwards.

Unfortunately, Kofoed was only a civilian employee. He did not have arresting power. But Kofoed despised Edwards. And, Edwards lacked a conscience. Edwards had no feelings and empathy toward the intense pain that Jessica's family and friends were enduring, day after day, not knowing what happened to her.

How did she die? Where was the murder weapon? Did Edwards dig a hole and bury her in a shallow grave out in the middle of nowhere? Could she have been weighted down and tossed into a river, a lake, or a creek? Foremost, how was her body moved away from her boyfriend's house? There were only two ways out of the downstairs basement bedroom. One way was through a storm window leading to the yard. But given its narrow width, there was no chance Edwards could lift his dead lover's body up through the storm window. That left the staircase as the only other option. Authorities determined Jessica was not buried in the crawl space or elsewhere in the multi-story home on North 130th Street.

In the days that followed, Edwards did not wilt under the unbelievable public pressure being cast upon him. To the sheriff's satisfaction, the pesky Omaha television news trucks continued to circle past Jane Edwards's normally quiet suburban neighborhood house nonstop. In spite of all this media hysteria, Edwards tried to go about his normal everyday life as cool, calm, and collected. But would he hold up? And would law enforcement carry through and arrest their prime suspect if Jessica's body was never located?

For Edwards, it was a waiting game. He waited to be arrested, but as time passed, he gained some confidence. He was well aware of the multiple murder cases around the country where frustrated authorities had to back off their suspect because the missing person's body failed to surface. Edwards was not running his mouth or blabbing about the circumstances of Jessica's murder to friends or coworkers. He kept everything all bottled up inside his head.

Absent an incriminating break down and tell-all confession, there was only one other way Edwards would be arrested and charged with Jessica's murder.

A lot more clues were needed, Kofoed determined.

* * *

After pulling an all-nighter searching for physical evidence at the suspect's home on May 16-17, Kofoed needed some rest. That meant turning over the forensics investigation to Connelly and one of his other ace pupils, CL Retelsdorf.

In 2006, Kofoed considered CL Retelsdorf and Josh Connelly as two of his favorite and most reliable employees. Kofoed had recruited both young men to come work with him after serving as their instructor at the Nebraska Wesleyan University forensics department in Lincoln.

These disciples of Kofoed were in his good graces, and they idolized their boss. In turn, Kofoed gave them higher pay grades and a lot more prestige and responsibilities than many of their other hard-working, more experienced peers in the lab. With Connelly and Retelsdorf, Kofoed liked their can-do attitude, their dedication to crime scene work, and that both young men were easy for him to manipulate.

And besides, Kofoed loved to surround himself with people of power. Retelsdorf's older sister, Leigh Ann, happened to be the chief criminal prosecutor for the Douglas County Attorney's Office. Leigh Ann handled the bulk of the trials involving high-profile Omaha-area murder cases. Over several years, Leigh Ann strung together an excellent record of success at the Douglas County Courthouse. She usually won her murder cases and became a highly regarded trial lawyer.

The report synopsis of both men's work stated that Sheriff's Capt. Dean Olson assigned them to process two vehicles for any evidence that could be related to Jessica's missing person case. Retelsdorf drew the task of searching the Honda CR-V owned by Jane

Edwards, while Connelly was told to inspect the suspect's car, the dark-colored Honda Accord. Both vehicles had been towed back to the sheriff's office for evidence processing.

Regarding the May 17 search of the aunt's vehicle, the CSI forensic report stated, "there was nothing of interest in the vehicle that was collected as evidence."

On the other hand, a concerted effort was made to carefully inspect the Honda car owned by the prime suspect. After all, it seemed far more likely Edwards used his own car – or Jessica's – to get rid of her body from his basement bedroom. However, the officials at the Douglas County Sheriff's Office did not give much credence to the later scenario. As Connelly dug through the suspect's car, he found a plethora of objects that required further analysis, items that did not necessarily seem to tie back to Jessica's murder and disposal, though. A Douglas County CSI report states that Connelly found several unopened bottles of Heineken beer. There were also T-shirts, straws, and trash in the car. A number of DVD movies and music CDs were strewn across the car, including music by the popular country band, Rascal Flatts, the Douglas County CSI unit's photos showed. The CSI report noted the recovery of a box of Pringles chips, fake Easter glass, a black necktie, and blue slippers within the suspect's backseat.

And there was also a book, which is praised by generations as the good book. Connelly removed a Bible which had Christopher Edwards's name engraved on the cover, according to the search warrant inventory of items retrieved.

As his day wore on, Connelly documented, photographed, and carefully removed each object from the interior of the suspect's car. Buried deep underneath a pile of junk in the backseat, Connelly retrieved a set of pruning shears, the CSI report stated. The CSI's photos showed the shears had long, wooden handles and sharp steel blades. They were a most unusual object to locate within the messy back seat of a 19-year-old young man under a cloud of suspicion for killing one of his girlfriends and successfully concealing the location of her body. Of course, the pruning shears were not the only unusual object in the suspect's backseat, according to CSI reports. A yellow shovel with its handle broken off was also discovered in the backseat. Connelly began his important assignment at 10:50 a.m., and he finished the task at 4:30 p.m., according to the CSI report.

He would have torn through every nook and cranny of the car. His forensic photos showed a car in total chaos just like the life of Edwards. Upon closer inspection, the square-pointed shovel was determined to contain river silt and grass. Connelly did not report finding any droplets of blood on the objects taken out of the backseat, such as the hedge shears and shovel. Once removed from the car, the hedge shears and shovel were moved into the crime lab's property and evidence division for safekeeping. But given the complete absence of blood on the metal blades, the hedge shears did not seem to factor into Jessica's death.

Connelly, like anybody tasked with investigating a bloody and vicious high-profile murder case, would know to give it his best effort. It did not take a brain surgeon to realize the most convenient place to conceal a dead body for disposal was the trunk. Only a crazed fool would toss a dead body into the passenger seat and then go driving aimlessly around trying to find a dump site. It stood to reason that Connelly paid keen attention to the interior and exterior of the suspect's car, including the trunk. After all, Connelly had no assurance that somebody else would even think to recheck his work at a later date. Normally, when the CSIs did not find any physical or trace evidence in a suspect's vehicle, their work was completed.

And since this was the biggest open case in Omaha, Connelly was on red alert to turn in his best performance. He was well aware that his agency had not yet arrested Edwards because investigators desired more clues to tie Edwards to Jessica's probable slaying.

Connelly had the backing and wholehearted support of his boss. Kofoed had the utmost confidence in Connelly's work after having taught Connelly. "I actually recruited Josh," Kofoed later told the *Omaha World-Herald* newspaper. "He was the best student I had. I was cherry-picking the students I wanted."

In the days ahead, a number of additional clues were about to start trickling out of the Douglas County crime lab to implicate Edwards. If these clues were authentic and on the up and up, then Kofoed's former star pupil apparently turned in a dismal performance when it mattered the most, during a day-long processing of the murder suspect's car.

Connelly did not report finding any blood stains in the vehicle including the most logical place to hide a body, the suspect's trunk. Connelly's work validated the previous night's effort back at the Edwards house, before the car was towed away and brought to Kofoed's crime lab.

Connelly's colleague, CSI Christine Gabig, had noted in her report how she inspected the trunk including a damaged tire left in the suspect's trunk. Her manual inspection of the debris in the trunk also failed to unearth any visible blood stains.

In essence, two different Douglas County CSIs, on separate assignments, went through Christopher Edwards's car. They inspected the car up close and personal. They removed various contents. Their own eyes were trained to spot blood. They saw none of it.

"Based on my recollections of what I remember, no, I don't remember finding or seeing blood," Connelly later testified.

* * *

Later that same day, Wednesday, May 17, Kofoed came back to the office refreshed and raring to go. He would have quickly realized the Edwards case had hit a giant snag. There were no blood stains, DNA, or trace evidence linking the car back to Jessica's murder. This was bad news to the boss. The long-term repercussions were quite unnerving. Edwards could roam free and thumb his nose at police. The crime lab's inability to tie the suspect's car back to the vicious, bloody crime scene might put an arrest in jeopardy.

Kofoed recognized it would be far more helpful to secure Edwards's arrest and conviction if more of Jessica's blood emerged. The trunk of the suspect's car seemed a most logical location to recover some fresh blood stains.

As the night wore on, most of Kofoed's CSIs had finished up their daily assignments and gone home for the evening, including the fatigued Connelly and Retelsdorf. As for Kofoed, he was preoccupied and consumed by Jessica's murder case. "I may not have left from (May) seventeenth on," Kofoed later testified. "I'm not sure. I may have been there continuously."

The rest of the sheriff's brass presumed Kofoed was a quintessential workaholic who liked to immerse himself in his forensics work.

As for Edwards's car, it remained under Kofoed's control, within the enclosed sally port not far from Kofoed's commander's office as well.

Kofoed did not need long to contemplate his next move. The car obviously needed another look.

* * *

Kofoed, almost age fifty, was no stranger to being backed into a corner and needing to come up with irrefutable, hard evidence to connect an obvious suspect to a brutal murder.

Only one month earlier, in April of 2006, Kofoed directed the crime scene investigation into the Murdock, Nebraska, bloody farmhouse killings of Wayne Stock, age 58, and his wife, Sharmon, age 55, an hour's drive from Omaha.

The shotgun slayings at point-blank range of both middle-aged victims were among the bloodiest murders Kofoed had processed in his law enforcement career. The farm couple's blood poured into their upstairs carpeting, and their blood sprayed their hallway walls. In that case, Kofoed was put under a lot of duress. The lead investigators from two different outside agencies had badgered Kofoed endlessly. There was no hard evidence to tie the killings back to the lead suspects, a pair of cousins.

That case preoccupied Kofoed's time, and it was happening less than a month before Jessica's disappearance back in Omaha. Finally, the Nebraska cousins were arrested and charged with the farmhouse killings. Kofoed learned one of them confessed and implicated the other as his accomplice. Kofoed decided to spring into action. He needed to be the hero. Before the arrests were made, Kofoed personally supervised an intensive eight-hour examination of a Ford Contour suspected as the cousins' getaway car in the late night farmhouse killings. During that first inspection, no blood, DNA, or trace evidence was found, and yet, the car still stayed under Kofoed's direct control. With the suspects in custody, Kofoed decided the alleged getaway car apparently warranted another look.

On the afternoon of April 27, Kofoed asked his trusty sidekick, CL Retelsdorf, to join him for a second search. This time, Kofoed emerged from underneath the dashboard of the tan Ford Contour. He acted excited as he held up a blood-stained piece of crime lab filter paper. He showed the specimen to his younger apprentice. Tests later confirmed Kofoed's filter paper contained a perfect DNA profile of farmhouse victim Wayne Stock. It was the only area of the car Kofoed chose to personally search that memorable afternoon.

Kofoed's discovery of the blood was the missing link the lead homicide investigators needed to sew up their case against the two jailed cousins.

And, it helped solidify Kofoed as a CSI genius until the next big case came along.

Chapter 7

Veteran Bill Kaufhold was the Douglas County crime lab's elder statesman with about twenty-five years on the force. Kaufhold had a reputation of being proficient, but he was not one to make waves or rock the boat. Unlike his boss, Kaufhold shunned the limelight and did not go out of his way to cozy up with the press.

If he had suspicions his boss was devious, Kaufhold was not going around the sheriff's department making such opinions known. Shortly after Kaufhold arrived to start his morning shift on May 18, 2006, commander Kofoed devised a top priority assignment to carry out right away. The clock was ticking.

Around 7:30 a.m., Kaufhold and his boss strolled over toward the area at the sheriff's office where Edwards's car was impounded.

Concentrate on the trunk and rear exterior of the vehicle, Kofoed relayed to his experienced subordinate.

Kaufhold panned the trunk. He looked over the exterior rear areas of the suspect's car in the spots where his boss urged Kaufhold to check. He definitely saw something. "Kaufhold located what appeared to be blood on the black colored, upper rubber trunk gasket towards the passenger side and the gray-colored metal interior upper trunk frame," Kaufhold stated in his report.

From there, the technician and commander Kofoed took several photographs showing the newly discovered red stains believed to be Jessica's blood.

"We found blood in the trunk of Chris's car on the gasket ... right underneath where you can't see it visibly," Kofoed would testify. "That was all identified as Jessica. She was transported, or items with her blood on them were transported, in the trunk of that car."

Indeed, two distinct red blood stains in different spots of the suspect's trunk had magically appeared.

"Similar to the vehicle search in the Murdock case, we examine and re-examine evidence and or vehicles based on some really common sense principles," Kofoed later explained. "The Edwards vehicle was initially examined at the scene. It was towed to (Douglas County Sheriff's Office) for further examination. There was no hunch. It was pretty much common sense. If Edwards removed her from the house in his vehicle, she would probably be placed in the trunk. To do a proper examination of the trunk, all areas of the trunk were required to be examined."

Kofoed reiterated his contention "it wasn't really a hunch" that blood would surface during the follow-up probe he conducted with Kaufhold.

"At a crime scene, you always have to remember to look up, whether it is the ceiling in the Chris Edwards bedroom or the trunk of his car," Kofoed explained. "Once, I was examining a body discovered in a drainage ditch below a tree. I looked up in the tree branches above the victim and to my surprise discovered the victim's purse hanging in the branches high above her. Weeks later, the suspect confessed. He stated that he threw the victim into the drainage ditch. Before he drove way, he flung her purse from the road toward her body. It ended up stuck in the tree above her."

Against Edwards, Kofoed's premonition produced visible blood stains in the only area of the vehicle ordered for a forensic inspection on the morning of May 18.

In essence, it was almost the same scenario that played itself out three weeks earlier during the Murdock farmhouse killings when forensic scientist CL Retelsdorf was summoned to accompany his boss along for a follow-up search of the suspected getaway car. In both unrelated murder cases, blood from the victim appeared in an odd and unorthodox place within the car. In Murdock, it surfaced under the dashboard. Against Edwards, the blood appeared on the top portion of the inside lid of his trunk. No blood showed up anywhere on the trunk carpet or anywhere else, such as where the tire rested, or on the tool pouch. On both occasions, it was commander Kofoed who had the amazing foresight to facilitate a follow-up forensic search in a lone specific area of the car where blood was then found.

Except this time around, a lot more blood was noticeable in the Edwards car, unlike the Murdock situation. "Both samples taken from the rubber gasket and trunk frame resulted in a positive result for blood," Kaufhold stated in his report.

During their fortuitous morning together, Kaufhold took photographs of his prima donna CSI boss crawling inside the suspect's trunk. There, Kofoed captured the haunting visuals of the newfound incriminating red stains.

The dramatic photos showing Kofoed inside the suspect's trunk would later turn into golden clues for trial. Kofoed rightfully sensed a jury would be captivated and spell bound by his incredible work ethic and penchant for detail as he doggedly investigated Jessica's homicide. That morning, the rubber gasket and interior upper frame of metal were also removed from the Honda Accord with special tools.

The pair of men finished their morning's task after about two and a half hours. Without a doubt, it was a most productive morning after the previous day's letdown by Josh Connelly, who had a master's degree in forensic science.

* * *

The task of transporting the blood stains from the trunk of Edwards's car might seem mundane. After all, it was a task a CSI rookie could execute. But in this case, it was a job that only the proud boss wanted to handle.

Kofoed delegated himself for this duty, a pattern that would be repeated again and again throughout the evidence-gathering build up to Edwards's arrest.

By early afternoon, Kofoed was cruising across Omaha with his two new bloody clues in tow.

In Omaha's Midtown neighborhood, the sheriff's commander pulled into the University of Nebraska Medical Center parking lot. He marched into the facility's DNA Laboratory to confer with medical technologist Melissa Helligso. She was a tanned, blonde knockout with short hair. She served as the Douglas County Sheriff's Office primary DNA consultant.

She and Kofoed had a close and personal friendship. That afternoon, Kofoed handed over his pair of red-stained clues to her care and custody. UNMC's third-party independent DNA lab would handle the swabbing and subsequent scientific tests for this and dozens of other clues that would be processed in Jessica's case.

It was a fruitful and most productive day at the Douglas County Sheriff's Office. The command staff was subsequently alerted to Kofoed's fabulous work of examining the suspect's trunk and finding some blood that day.

The incriminating clues in Edwards's trunk definitely caused a spike in the confidence level within the sheriff's office. Without the trunk blood, it would be hard to convince a judge and jury that Jessica's body was ever moved away from outside of the Edwards property. In actual size, the blood stains were small. In the totality of the forensic evidence, the blood stains in the trunk were huge, almost as important as the bloody mattress itself.

But the blood in the trunk just wasn't enough—for the time being—to make an arrest.

* * *

May 22 marked the seventh day the sheriff's office CSI unit was in hot pursuit of apprehending Jessica's killer. This was a CSI case pure and simple. The success or failure of the investigation rested squarely on the shoulders of Kofoed and the ambition of his highly competent forensic unit.

For the time being, Chris Edwards was still out walking the streets of Omaha, able to relish his freedom. By early afternoon, Kofoed had pulled out the pair of wooden-handled hedge shears from the evidence unit. At 1:30 p.m., he proceeded to personally escort the sharp instrument over to the University of Nebraska Medical Center. There, he gave them to Melissa Helligso. When the hedge shears was removed from the backseat of Edwards's car almost a week earlier, the forensic report chronicling Josh Connelly's work made no mention that the hedge shears contained any evidence. In spite of that, Kofoed had the shears tested for DNA at the UNMC laboratory. Helligso administered rubbing swabs on the object and then handed the shears back to Kofoed. The forensic report plainly states Kofoed retained possession of the hedge shears and returned them back to his Douglas County Sheriff's Office.

It's hard to say what was going through Kofoed's head at this time, but it's clear the sheriff's office intended to identify a murder weapon to use against Edwards. With no weapon, the prosecutor's office might decide to pass altogether on charging Edwards with murder. Then, at 8 a.m. on May 24, just two days after Kofoed personally brought the hedge shears to UNMC, Kofoed summoned CSI Michelle Steele Potter re-check the hedge shears, along with the yellow shovel also found a full week earlier in the suspect's backseat. She carried out the assignment in two-and-a-half hours. In summary, Potter collected four separate swab boxes of the shovel and pruning shears. Her report stated the evidence would remain in the property and evidence division. She also conducted several tests on the shovel and shears trying to recover latent fingerprints. No latent prints were developed.

Six days later, Kofoed was back at it again. At 8:30 a.m. May 30, he drove across town back to see Melissa Helligso at UNMC's DNA laboratory. This time, he bundled up plenty of evidence for the drive including clues with obvious drenched blood. He included the two blood-soaked towels he found on the night the mattress was recovered. For Kofoed, now was the perfect time to transport the buccal swabs taken from suspect Christopher Edwards, along with a buccal swab obtained from Bob Edwards, the suspect's dad. The swab boxes recovered from the pruning shears and shovel were also delivered to UNMC.

The case against Christopher Edwards was heating up. Curiously, something had possessed Kofoed to decide to revisit those shears. Now, he was personally hand delivering the garden tools back to UNMC for yet a second time.

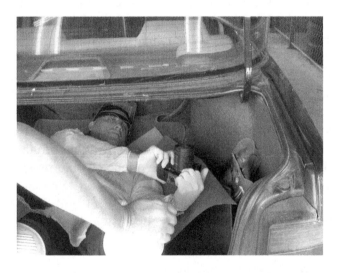

After forensic scientist Josh Connelly's failed search for Jessica's blood, Douglas County CSI Commander David Kofoed decided to recheck the trunk of the suspect's car the very next morning. This time, visible blood stains were found in two different spots of the upper portion of Edwards' trunk.

Chapter 8

Averaging thirty to forty murder cases every year in Omaha, the Douglas County prosecutor's office tended to push murder cases with so-so evidence to the backburner. Those crimes were pursued when evidence became stronger, a year or two down the road, or maybe never.

But Kofoed was persistent. He would not stand for letting Jessica's murder turn into a cold case. Omaha demanded justice for Jessica. The bloodbath in the suspect's room only fueled the CSI commander's motivation to dig up more clues to ensure Edwards's guilt.

* * *

As each day in May passed, the saga surrounding the charming coed's shocking mysterious disappearance remained Omaha's top news story.

The Jessica O'Grady story often led the noon, dinner, and nightly television news broadcasts. The general consensus was that Jessica met her untimely demise at the hands of her lover, Edwards. But at least three nagging questions remained unanswered: Where did Jessica's killer put her body? What was his weapon? When, if ever, might Edwards face murder charges?

Not surprisingly, some people figured unless Jessica's body washed up or turned up in a field or a ditch, her unscrupulous boyfriend was in the clear. Skeptics presumed that without a body, the prosecution had no case. At that moment, there had never been a jury conviction involving a no-body murder trial across Nebraska.

But CSI Kofoed was not one of those naysayers.

Three years earlier, he had gained an incredible wealth of experience and fame for his role investigating Ivan Henk, a notorious child murderer in Plattsmouth, Nebraska, a city of 7,000 about twenty miles from Omaha. Little Brendan Gonzalez's horrendous murder marked another occasion where the CSI commander from Douglas County arrived to help a small-town police department in a time of great struggle. Some of the key facts were indisputable.

The psychopath Henk murdered his little four-year-old son, Brendan. After Henk committed the murder, he successfully hid the little boy's body as a crude and disgusting way to taunt Brendan's distraught mother, Rebecca Gonzalez.

Little Brendan's murder mystery was a lot like Jessica's case. Hundreds of volunteers and concerned residents from Nebraska came out in droves. They searched ditches, culverts, and wildlife sanctuaries across the mostly rural Cass County and neighboring Sarpy County trying to find Brendan's remains. One of the nearby regional dumps, the Sarpy County Landfill near Springfield, Nebraska, underwent numerous searches for Brendan's body. But nobody had any luck.

Meanwhile, confessed killer Ivan Henk continued to smirk and gloat about the murder. One time, Henk even boasted in an open courtroom, packed with several news media present, that he had murdered his own son. Henk made outlandish and preposterous statements claiming he killed his peaceful and smiling four-year-old son because the boy was really Satan, the Anti-Christ, and that the boy had the mark of Satan, the 6-6-6, across his forehead. Henk was crazy and manipulative, but he was found to be sane, and rightfully so. Frustrated, the Nebraska authorities kept him jailed on unrelated charges for months as they tried in vain to recover Brendan's body, but time was running out.

The prosecutor from Cass County did not want to jeopardize a conviction against Henk by filing murder charges prematurely. The residents of Cass County would revolt if a sicko like Henk was released from jail due to insufficient evidence. In the Brendan Gonzalez murder case, part of that uphill battle facing Nebraska law enforcement was the absence of Brendan's body. The Plattsmouth police needed to prove Henk committed murder. And that's essentially how a shadowy figure like Kofoed emerged and came to save the day in a miraculous fashion for the

Plattsmouth Police Department.

As the case entered its sixth month, in June of 2003, Ivan Henk decided to lead the weary police investigators on a wild goose chase. A police convoy headed north to the neighboring city of Bellevue, not far from the sprawling Offutt Air Force base. On a whim, the proud and manipulative child killer pointed to a Dumpster outside a ratty apartment complex. There, Henk claimed he had disposed of his slain little boy some five months earlier during broad day light.

Taking Henk at his word, the authorities impounded the Dumpster and brought it back to the Plattsmouth city garage. That afternoon, Kofoed was notified, and he leaped into action. He hopped into the CSI van and brought along his sidekick CL Retelsdorf. After making the thirty-minute drive, Kofoed and his partner set up a video camera in Plattsmouth. They filmed themselves sifting through the garbage debris, piece by piece, as officers with the Plattsmouth Police Department hovered around them.

That day, after the video camera was turned off, a bunch of debris was brought back to the Douglas County crime lab in Omaha under the guise of further analysis. A day or two later, Kofoed pulled one of his all-time best magic acts. He was Harry Houdini and David Copperfield rolled into one. With nobody else around at his crime lab, Kofoed claimed he conducted his forensic tests upon some of the junk recovered from the bowels of the smelly and disgusting commercial trash bin. Kofoed relayed that his crime lab filter paper received a strong reaction for the presence of blood. From there, Kofoed sent his blood-stained filter papers over to the University of Nebraska Medical Center in Omaha. Amazingly, his filter papers came back with a full and complete DNA profile of the boy, Brendan Gonzalez. This was some five months after the dead boy was supposedly put into the outdoor trash bin by Henk.

Next, Kofoed alerted the prosecutor in Plattsmouth, the Plattsmouth Police Department, and the Nebraska State Patrol investigators of his uncanny discovery. The presence of the murder victim's blood inside a Dumpster might seem insignificant to outside bystanders, but it was a tipping point in the murder case for tactical reasons. The previously cautious prosecutor soon moved forward with a first-degree murder charge against Henk. The charge carried a possible death penalty. Eventually, Henk pleaded guilty to murdering his son in exchange for a life sentence.

Sadly, Brendan's mother still grieves to this day, not knowing where her son's body is at. Brendan's remains have never been found.

* * *

From the Henk murder case, Kofoed realized if given the chance to reprocess a crime scene over and over, he should take it.

Ordinarily, police departments worth their weight in gold don't go back a second or third time to reprocess a crime scene for clues they supposedly missed the first time. Besides, rarely does the criminal justice system afford the police a rain check to go back into the suspect's private property, again and again, just because the police thought they missed a spot.

But Jessica O'Grady's May 2006 disappearance was not a normal Omaha murder case. It had ascended to the top of the news casts. The sheriff's office knew it had a guilty suspect floating around the community. Omaha would not stand a scenario in which Edwards could skate past the tentacles of the justice system much longer.

Meanwhile, Kofoed's agency remained antsy. Without a body, authorities could not show a court how Jessica had died. The prosecution needed more to ensure a conviction. The recovery of a medieval and barbaric weapon would be a nice start to reenergize the murder investigation of Edwards.

Kofoed knew it would be incredibly impressive to uncover a mesmerizing clue to overshadow the Omaha police's recovery of the giant blood-soaked mattress.

It did not take too much arm twisting for Kofoed to convince his direct supervisor, Captain Dean Olson, to let him go back into the home of Edwards, a second time, to execute another search warrant. At the time, Kofoed was rather fortunate that Olson was a faithful and ardent cheerleader for all that was happening under Kofoed's leadership. Thanks to his marketing prowess, Kofoed was keeping the- county's crime lab in the constant limelight.

A second crack at the Edwards home would give the CSI unit a chance to make a giant splash. Maybe a glamorous and convenient weapon would be hauled away. But why would the murder weapon still be present inside the suspect's bedroom? Surely Edwards knew he was under the thumb of the police. They had raided his home a week earlier and removed the blood-soaked mattress. That initial search, lasting from midnight until mid-morning, did not locate Jessica's body nor the weapon used to kill her. It seemed obvious the weapon was long gone, just like Jessica's skeletal remains. Edwards likely got rid of the weapon as fast as he disposed of poor defenseless Jessica. He had no incentive to keep the weapon around and every incentive to destroy it.

But how and where would the sheriff's office come up with a murder weapon several days after Jessica's disappearance?

Investigators applied the heat to Edwards's friends.

Among other things, Edwards's long-time high school friend and golfing buddy, Riley Wasserburger, revealed Edwards owned a matching set of Bangkok battle swords. The swords were each about eighteen inches in length with black grip handles. The silver blades contained a sharp point. Wasserburger remembered the swords were kept in Edwards's bedroom closet. He told the sheriff's office he saw Edwards displaying the swords about a month prior to Jessica's homicide. Kofoed knew a lot about ceremonial swords himself. His own office at the Douglas County Sheriff's Office was decorated with lots of Marine Corps memorabilia including a large impressive saber.

The sheriff's office decided to roll ahead with a second search warrant to be executed within the Edwards home after darkness fell.

"Searches of the residence by OPD and DCSO investigators on May 17, 2006, did not uncover the swords, which are viewed as potential murder weapons in this homicide," stated the warrant drawn up by sheriff's investigator William Rinn.

The judge who rubber-stamped the search warrant for approval did not grill the sheriff's office to explain a most obvious question: How and why did the Douglas County CSI team manage to overlook the pair of Bangkok battle swords if they were meticulously tearing through the Edwards bedroom less than one week earlier, spending eight to ten hours inside the home?

Nevertheless, Douglas County Judge Stephen Swartz approved the search warrant. The raid would be conducted during the night time hours of May 22, 2006.

The crime lab commander could not have been more pleased.

Kofoed's team got a second crack at inspecting the Edwards home to dig up more clues. This was a huge opportunity, and Kofoed would be right there in the middle, spearheading the forensic search. "This is an unusual case," Kofoed later testified. "I'd done one other case where we never recovered a body and that was Brendan Gonzalez, and I learned a lot from that experience. You learn things you would have rather done, and so I said, 'We need to go back and get that section (of ceiling).'"

After the Douglas County Sheriff's Office stormed the home of Chris Edwards for a second full-blown raid, Omaha defense lawyer James Martin Davis drove over to the property, to keep his clients' emotions in check.

"Kofoed was there, and all of the TV stations were out there," Davis recalled, "and there was a lot of video cameras. I tried to keep both Bob (Edwards) and Chris out of the limelight."

Later on, Kofoed claimed his primary reason for desiring to poke around the Edwards home a second time was to re-inspect the suspect's garage. "I thought it was significant that we had not found anything, and you know, it's not just to prove the positive, it's to prove the negative, you know, I want to positively know that something doesn't exist so I want to go back and again, just process that garage floor again," Kofoed testified.

Conversely, Kofoed was one of roughly a dozen law enforcement personnel to canvass the suspect's multi-story home on the first night of the police probe. They all saw the same things. They did not spot any blood in the garage. So what were Kofoed's true motivations for going back into the suspect's home a second time? Did the commander have devious and deliberate intentions? Was he fueled by his desire to stand on top of his state's forensic community pedestal, where he would be revered by his professional peers and idolized by his master's degree level students at the Nebraska Wesleyan University where he also taught forensics?

Chapter 9

The idea Edwards used his ceremonial battle swords to slay his lover would go down as the most controversial and widely talked about clue of Jessica's murder case.

The motive of the crime was apparent. Edwards killed Jessica in gruesome fashion because he did not want to be the father of babies from two different girlfriends at the same time. He saw the merits of a long-term relationship with Michelle. The idea of a long-term romance with Jessica detested him.

Mostly, he did not want Jessica to ruin his life, his future. As a consequence, he made sure she was no longer a member of the human race. Then he got rid of her.

And, he was also the kind of weasel to cover his tracks and try to stay one step ahead of the cops. When it came to the bloody carnage in his bedroom, Edwards took action to remedy the situation. He bought the cleaning fluids at Walgreens the day after Jessica went missing. He brushed the white shoe polish and other white chemical fluids over the fresh specks of blood spatter above his bed on the ceiling.

But Edwards made a terrible blunder. He failed to recognize the tenacious Omaha Police detectives were hot on his case and about to show up unannounced a few days later with discerning intentions of searching the home.

From that point on, Edwards could have known his arrest was imminent. It could happen any day.

In Edwards's mind, the ceremonial swords would be of no concern. Obviously, he knew the truth. Besides, these swords were just a set of play toys. Prior to Jessica's murder, he showed them off to his friends. He pulled them out in front of his true girlfriend, Michelle Wilken. Then, he put them back in the closet.

He never fathomed his Bangkok battle swords would be scooped up and heralded as the elusive murder weapon used to hack Jessica to death.

But they were. They would become a lasting dark footnote in Omaha's true-crime history—one of the most infamous murder clues ever displayed in an Omaha murder case.

Late into the night, around 11:45 p.m., on May 22, 2006, a matching pair of ceremonial swords, wrapped in a set of black nylon sheaths, was paraded out of his home by a team of sheriff's investigators helping Kofoed.

Deputy Tom Walter had the distinction of finding them. That night, he handed them over to Deputy Brenda Wheeler. From there, the swords were returned to the sheriff's office. They were moved into the crime lab's property and evidence unit for safekeeping and storage.

"The sword gained a lot of attention with the media," Kofoed remembered.

Back in 2006, during Kofoed's heyday, the retrieval of the ceremonial swords was the equivalent of holding up the elusive Super Bowl's Lombardi Trophy. The mere sight of the swords would leave jurors spellbound and mortified.

Behind the scenes, the recovery of the sword signaled a tremendous turning point. Jessica's case was coming together as anticipated. But a sword absent of Jessica's blood would be of no help at all to the investigation.

* * *

The chance to revisit the Edwards home after dark was not just about finding the alleged murder weapons. Among the other CSIs present was Bill Kaufhold, the same technician summoned to help Kofoed spot the blood stains in the suspect's trunk five days before.

Down in the basement, Kaufhold was assigned to cut away two separate sections of ceiling tile. In the northeast corner of Edwards's bedroom, Kaufhold removed a piece that measured eighteen inches by

John Ferak

twenty-eight inches. Another section that was taken away measured forty inches by twenty inches.

The chunks of ceiling tiles were returned to the crime lab where they stayed under Kofoed's control and custody. On the overhead ceiling directly above his bed, Edwards was thought to have painted over the blood that sprayed out of Jessica at the time of her death.

Back at the crime lab, Kofoed was working alone, handling the sections of ceiling. All of a sudden, something happened. Kofoed alerted everyone in the unit that he had an error.

"I was swabbing the ceiling section which was painted over by the defendant. And I could tell there was blood underneath it, so I had to use a lot of friction and my glove ripped," Kofoed later told Omaha's WOWT television station.

In any event, the mischievous CSI commander claimed this accidental episode caused his own skin to make contact with one of his testing swabs.

If Kofoed was up to something sinister, he would not have wanted to take the gamble that Edwards's defense lawyers would get a hold of this contaminated filter paper swab with Kofoed's DNA. Kofoed would have stayed one step ahead of the game. He would never want the defense raising suspicion or casting doubt he might be tampering with the ceiling tiles as part of a scheme to add to the mounting evidence pile.

Therefore, the torn rubber glove needed to work as a perfect cover story.

"I knew I had exposed my own DNA to the swab itself," Kofoed later testified. "But I wasn't going to throw the swab away so I submitted it as evidence."

Ordinarily, someone in CSI would just throw away their glove. They would know their collected sample was not reliable, well-known Nebraska criminal defense lawyer Jerry Soucie explained.

"There was no reason to even submit the sample for DNA analysis," Soucie said. "There were multiple swab samples from the ceiling tiles collected by Kofoed that could be used. That's the fishy part—submitting a sample when he knew he had contaminated the swab, not the tearing of the glove."

Indeed, Kofoed was never questioned as far as how his rubber glove to ward off contamination apparently ripped in the first place. His colleagues just took him at his word and didn't blink an eye.

Mysteriously, Kofoed's torn glove – which should have also been contaminated as well – was never submitted to the University of Nebraska Medical Center DNA lab for testing. Rather, Kofoed submitted ten separate blood spots supposedly taken from cut out sections of the suspect's ceiling tiles. Nine of the ten spots were identified as having a positive DNA confirmation for Jessica's blood.

As for the infamous tenth sample, blood spot 799-FF also contained a positive reaction for blood. But that sample was given a bold black diamond on page three of Mellissa Helligso's sixteen-page DNA report: "Identified as Douglas County Sheriff's Office law enforcement personnel, and excluded from DNA report," she wrote.

Kofoed was in the clear. And the prosecutor's office had another building block of evidence to showcase for trial.

By self-reporting his error, Kofoed received high praise for taking the initiative to alert others in law enforcement to his apparent forensic mistake back in the lab.

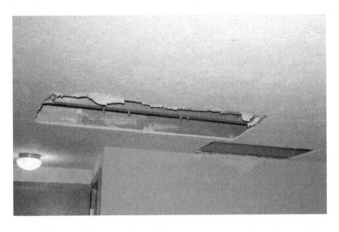

CSI Commander Kofoed said one of his primary goals for searching the Edwards home a second time was to remove a section of the ceiling tiles where Edwards had painted over various blood stains.

Chapter 10

Figuring there was a huge breaking development, the news media went wild when Kofoed's CSI posse executed the second raid at Jane Edwards's home during the late night hours of May 22-23, 2006. But the reporters left feeling a little betrayed because the night came and went without an arrest.

What the press did not know and therefore did not report at the time was that attorney James Martin Davis was involved in serious negotiations with the Douglas County authorities on behalf of his client, Chris Edwards.

Davis said he realized that working out a plea bargain was in his client's best interest. A short to moderate prison term was better than the alternative.

On May 23, Davis said, he began what turned into a daylong series of back and forth telephone conversations with Leigh Ann Retelsdorf, Douglas County's chief criminal prosecutor. "I got a call from Leigh Ann and she wanted to know if my client would cooperate," Davis recalled. "Leigh Ann and I had a mutual respect. I had been involved with dozens and dozens of cases with her previously."

Davis knew he had some leverage to work out a deal that might be advantageous to Chris Edwards, who still had not been charged with a crime.

"Since it was a no-body case, there was not enough evidence at this point to charge Chris with first-degree degree murder," Davis explained.

Davis said he was able to negotiate a compromise with the prosecutor's office to resolve the violent crime quickly. Chris Edwards would plead guilty to felony manslaughter under the condition he led authorities from the Douglas County Sheriff's Office to the recovery of the Jessica's remains. If the sheriff's office found the remains beforehand, "all bets on the deal were off," Davis noted.

"I was not trying to exploit the situation," Davis continued, "but the (O'Grady) family was willing to go along with that because they wanted a decent burial for their daughter, and they were willing to consider the lesser charge. We agreed if Chris would offer to disclose where Jessica was, that the charge would be reduced to manslaughter."

Sheriff Dunning remembered that the negotiations involving Davis and Douglas County authorities seemed productive. It appeared the case might be solved quickly, without any need for a prolonged and expensive trial.

Davis presumed that everybody was on board with the plea agreement.

He was badly mistaken. The suspect's father, Bob Edwards, was adamantly opposed to the prospect of his son pleading guilty to manslaughter, even if the charge only carried a maximum prison term of twenty years.

"I thought we had the deal done after I went and met with the sheriff," Davis said. "When I came back, the father just said he was getting somebody else. He hired me and in effect, fired me. By firing me, he, in effect, put any plea bargain agreement off the table."

***

A few days later, Douglas County Sheriff Tim Dunning predicted Jessica would not be found alive.

"We're not going to rush our investigation," Dunning told the *Omaha World-Herald* in a story published May 27, 2006.

The suspect, the sheriff asserted, remained under constant law enforcement surveillance. Authorities made sure Edwards would not flee Omaha. He was essentially a prisoner in his own home. On top of that, his transportation options were severely limited because his Honda Accord had been impounded.

"We know where he is, and we're always going to know where he is," Dunning assured the media.

As May came to a close, Kofoed and his crime lab

were in slow-down mode. This was not the kind of apathy one might expect from a highly regarded CSI commander who took pride for being obsessive compulsive and a quintessential workaholic, notably when it came to cracking major murder cases.

After all, Edwards was still free. No arrests had been made.

In any event, Kofoed and his crime lab were not displaying a gung-ho attitude when it came to getting a clear answer on the purported murder weapon, the infamous Bangkok battle sword. The lack of urgency surrounding the testing of the suspected weapon was a bit mystifying.

After all, the sooner the swords were tested for blood, the sooner the authorities could arrest Edwards for murder. Likewise, if the swords were excluded, authorities could pursue other possible leads and theories as well.

* * *

It is entirely possible Kofoed and his CSIs simply forgot about the sword tests. After all, this was an active, busy, and fast-paced murder probe.

Besides seizing the swords, a handful of small knives were also confiscated during the second property search. If none of these objects contained blood of the murder victim, the sheriff's office might have hit a brick wall. The absence of a definitive weapon and the unknown placement of Jessica's body might have forced the prosecutor's office to delay charging

Edwards with killing Jessica.

This would not have sat well with Jessica's distraught family and her many supporters. They had vigorously courted the media to force the police to make her case a high priority.

The mattress and trunk blood were solid clues to make an arrest, but perhaps not strong enough on their own to secure a murder conviction, where a jury verdict must be unanimous. The threshold in criminal court was beyond a reasonable doubt. The Edwards case was still a tad shaky for the prosecutor's office to charge.

Inexplicably, the pair of battle swords thought to be the murder weapon began to languish and collect dust. More than a week passed and still the swords had not been processed in the CSI's chemistry lab. Kofoed refrained from intervening and assigning someone to check the swords. Looking back, it would not be beyond the realm of possibilities for Kofoed to have delayed the forensics testing because he was planning something grand, dark, and mischievous. That way, he could let one of his favorite CSI employees share in the glory of the find. Such employees were part of his tight inner circle better known as "Team David." They were his sheep. He was their shepherd. He was blindly leading them astray.

It was a sick and twisted charade, but that's how he functioned during his rollercoaster tenure as the rogue lab manager.

It was around midnight, on May 31, when one of Kofoed's favorite CSI employees, Christine Gabig walked into the crime lab. She intended to photograph and conduct trace evidence tests on a number of possible weapons in Jessica's homicide.

Two of the potential murder weapons were wrapped in a set of black-colored mesh sheaths. These items were the pair of Bangkok battle swords that had been removed from the suspect's closet nine days earlier.

In her forensic report, Gabig stated her assignment to test the swords came from sheriff's investigator William Rinn way back on May 23. However, her report made no mention why she waited nine days to fulfill the work or why Kofoed, as commander, was acting disinterested in examining the possible weapons. After all, the primary reason to raid the Edwards home for the second time, according to court documents signed by the Douglas County judge, was to retrieve the pair of swords believed to be the murder weapon.

As she hunkered down for her task, the weight of the case rested on Christine Gabig's shoulders. In front of her, she had four black mesh sheaths. Gabig cut the sheaths open. She inspected them for blood and other trace evidence. Her testing results were negative, she noted in her forensic report. However, her forensic work in the chemistry lab was hardly done.

She still had in front of her three smaller-sized silver knives and two longer swords with blades measuring more than eighteen inches long.

It was now time to inspect the set of knives and the pair of swords.

Chapter 11

From midnight until 2:30 a.m., Christine Gabig conducted her all-important presumptive blood tests on the three smaller knives. None gave off a reaction for blood. She moved on. The pair of swords was up next on her exam table. Gabig could easily tell that both had shown use. She saw stains and scratches on the blades.

"No areas were visually identified as apparent bloodstains," Gabig stated.

And yet a tiny speck of invisible blood was found after the forensic scientist ran a cotton swab along one of the instruments. "A swab that was used on the edge of one of the swords tested positive with Phenolphthalein," Gabig's forensic report stated. Phenolphthalein was the chemical commonly applied by the CSI division when conducting presumptive blood tests. For instance, a pink reaction upon a piece of crime lab filter paper or a swab signified the likely presence of human blood.

As she worked the overnight shift, Gabig marked an X on the sword's handle. That let others know which side of the blade reacted for blood. She recommended that the sword should undergo DNA analysis, according to her report.

Talk about a huge breakthrough.

Indeed, a particle of dried blood had turned up on Douglas County's suspected murder weapon. The CSI team came through in the clutch. Kofoed's unit found the necessary smoking gun to sew up the investigation against Edwards.

Kofoed would be able to prop up Gabig as a shining star. There was proof of blood on the suspected murder weapon. Hours later, Kofoed began to take a keen interest in the sword. By 9 a.m., he met with sheriff's investigator Jennifer Tinsley, according to court records. He asked her to drive the sword over to the University of Nebraska Medical Center DNA lab. Later that same day, Kofoed was busy handling other blood specimens connected with Jessica's murder. He personally transported several swabs of mattress blood over to the same DNA lab for confirmatory testing.

Because authorities did not have Jessica's body, they needed to get creative to obtain her DNA samples. Otherwise they could never prove the blood on the mattress was Jessica's blood, and their murder case would be in serious jeopardy. At her apartment, authorities had retrieved a hairbrush, her underwear, and her shaving razor to obtain a DNA sample to compare against the bloody mattress. As widely anticipated, the DNA samples were a match.

The pieces of the murder mystery puzzle had come together in record time for a rare no-body murder case: only a matter of weeks. The tiny blood particle on the suspect's sword was the ultimate blow against Edwards. Despite the absence of Jessica's body, the evidence trove against him piled up quickly.

Now it wouldn't be long before Edwards's days and nights of freedom were over.

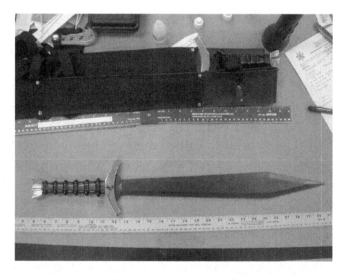

Douglas County CSI Christine Gabig reported how she found a tiny speck of blood on the tip of this battle sword after the object had been kept in the county crime lab for several days prior.

Chapter 12

The Douglas County Sheriff's Office made sure a full house of eager and hungry journalists assembled when Omaha's most despised murder suspect turned himself in on the afternoon of June 9, 2006.

Edwards was arrested on suspicion of homicide and use of a weapon to commit a felony. His life would never be the same, but at least he had a future. Jessica's life was cut short. She died way too young. She was robbed of her innocence, her charming personality, and gorgeous smile. In time, she might have found her Mr. Right. She could have settled down, matured, married, and had children. After all, Jessica loved kids.

But Jessica did not live to see her twentieth birthday. And now, her cheating boyfriend, the last person to see her alive, was finally being charged with her heinous death.

At the press conference to announce the arrest, Douglas County Chief Deputy Sheriff Marty Bilek expressed confidence in trying Edwards for Jessica's homicide in spite of the continued absence of her body.

"I can tell you that if we didn't have some certainty that she was deceased, then we wouldn't be filing some form of homicide against Chris Edwards," Bilek told the throng of pesky journalists.

The tragic culmination of events that resulted in the arrest of Edwards came as quite a shock for Chayse Bates, Jessica's former serious boyfriend during 2004 -2005. "I was not aware of anyone she was dating after we broke up," Bates remembered. "I never even heard of Christopher Edwards before it all happened. I honestly hoped she was doing OK in her life. Nothing in my mind can even conceive of doing what he did."

In any event, the time had arrived for Edwards to face the music for taking the life of Jessica in such a cruel and wicked fashion. His days of golfing, playing tennis with friends, tending bar, or shacking up with his multiple girlfriends were all a thing of the past.

At the time of his arrest for killing Jessica, Edwards had no prior criminal history, and he was only nineteen. By this time, the defendant's family had completely severed ties with media darling defense lawyer James Martin Davis. For the time being, they found someone less skilled to represent Chris and address the overzealous Omaha press corps clamoring for sound bites.

"His life has been put on hold," Omaha lawyer Matt

Higgins told reporters. "Not only is he an innocent man, he acts like an innocent man."

In the eyes of everyone closely monitoring the case, Higgins made a giant fool of himself with such outlandish statements in the press. Higgins had sought to portray his client as the victim of a wrongful prosecution.

On the contrary, the good people of Omaha did not feel sorry for Edwards. The law-abiding residents knew all too well that Edwards was their enemy. His arrest was met with great relief and sincere gratitude by Jessica's friends and family.

But their lives would never be the same either. They agonized. They were sad, distressed. Their world was fractured and torn apart. Making matters worse, they didn't have a proper place to grieve. Nobody knew what Edwards had done with Jessica's corpse. The cunning killer was keeping his lips sealed and showing no hint of giving a full confession. Edwards was content to let Jessica's friends and family remain flustered. He robbed them of the dignity of giving Jessica a proper funeral and burial.

"If he wants to completely cooperate with our office," Chief Deputy Sheriff Marty Bilek told the news media, "we would like him to tell us the whereabouts of Jessica O'Grady, and he has not done that yet. Until he does that, I won't consider him to be cooperating with us."

Over at the county crime lab, Kofoed was equally satisfied with the major developments as well. Surely, he knew the blood droplets he found all over the suspect's ceiling, plus the blood stains in the trunk, and the recent emergence of the sword would spell disaster for Edwards.

As the days and nights passed, Edwards would grow accustomed to wearing the orange, jail jumpsuit issued by the Douglas County jail in downtown Omaha. He would spend his days and nights in quiet, solemn reflection for his mortal sins. The massive Omaha jail housed more than a thousand prisoners at any given time. Edwards knew he could expect to stay in jail until his case went to trial. Jailers at the rough and tough corrections facility later told Omaha's television stations that Edwards was prone to spending his lonely days and nights alone in his cell, often crying.

He had plenty of time to rethink his wicked ways that robbed the world of a wonderful and beautiful young woman.

* * *

During the summer of 2006, Edwards's long divorced parents were reluctantly brought together by a common and unfortunate bond. They wanted their son to avoid a lifetime in a Nebraska maximum security prison. They went to bat for their son and remained faithfully in his corner. They wanted people to believe he was still a good son, that Jessica's murder was just a figment of peoples' imagination.

As time marched on, the lurid and haunting details of Jessica's demise stayed bottled up inside the crazed mind of the Omaha teenager who once was active in his Omaha church but was now a darkened villain, a soldier for Satan.

But being arrested and being convicted of murder were two different spectrums. Edwards would still get his day in court. He and his new team of lawyers had many months to prepare a defense. They would make it their mission to speculate that Jessica was not really dead, that she simply chose to disappear and drop out of sight.

* * *

One of the nation's leading experts on no-body murder cases said that some aspects of the Jessica O'Grady homicide in Nebraska were the exception to the rule. Oftentimes, no-body murder cases can take seven to ten years before they are solved, explained attorney Thomas "Tad" DiBiase.

DiBiase worked as a federal prosecutor in the District of Columbia for more than twelve years. The former Brooklyn Law School graduate has tried at least twenty murder cases before a jury, including one no-body case. He has researched the phenomenon of no-body murder cases and maintains an active website at www.nobodymurdercases.com. In 2014, DiBiase published the book, *No-Body Homicide Cases: A Practical Guide to Investigating, Prosecuting and Winning Cases When the Victim is Missing*.In Jessica's case, the Douglas County Sheriff's Office moved forward and charged Edwards only a month after she went missing.

"That was very bold on their part," DiBiase said of the Douglas County Sheriff's Office arrest. "A lot of times, they tend to hold off an arrest until you find a body. It's always better to have a body."

With Edwards, authorities were obviously "confident that they had the right person" to sustain a conviction at trial, DiBiase noted. "At the end of the day, that is still a huge risk on their part because you only get one shot at all."

As of May 25, 2015, DiBiase has confirmed there have been at least 444 no-body murder trials in the U.S. Based on his findings, convictions in no-body murders cases tend to happen about 88 percent of the time. The other 12 percent, roughly 50 such cases, resulted in dismissals, mistrials, acquittals, or conviction reversals on appeal. About 91 percent of all such cases involved male defendants and 58 percent of the victims were females—the same circumstances of the Jessica O'Grady tragedy.

Most no-body murder cases have one of more of these factors: forensic evidence, a confession to a friend, or a confession to police. The Edwards case had only one of the three: the forensic evidence. "In these cases, DNA evidence is the best evidence to have," DiBiase explained, from the prosecution's purview.

In all likelihood, Edwards removed his victim's body from his bedroom during the night of his crime, DiBiase said.

"Otherwise, the body starts to break down and

decompose, and it becomes very smelly," DiBiase said. "The most common way to get rid of a body is having it buried in the ground. With water, unless you weigh it down, eventually it tends to float to the top." Contrary to popular belief, most no-body killers don't bury their victim far away from the site of the crime. These killers tend to avoid hauling the body out to a remote distant land that would involve trespassing, DiBiase explained.

"It's usually done at a location that is familiar to the suspect," DiBiase said. "The person is not going to go to a place that is strange. Plus, it takes time to dig. The last thing they want to do is cause someone else to see them with a body."

Often, the killer selects a site where he can still monitor the burial from a distance and the police activities after the act. "Very often, they want to keep track. Are the police going there to dig?" DiBiase pointed out.

Some characteristics of the Edwards murder case have common traits to many other no-body murders, DiBiase explained.

About 52 percent of all no-body tragedies involve a domestic relationship -- just as Jessica O'Grady's murder -- where the crime involved a boyfriend and a girlfriend, DiBiase noted in his database. Many such murders happen in a bedroom, when nobody else was around.

"These are very common indoors, and it generally always happens when there are no other witnesses present," DiBiase said.

"These are often crimes of passion and crimes of control and doing this (hiding the body) is the ultimate act of control."

About a month after Jessica disappeared without a trace, the Douglas County Sheriff's Office charged Christopher Edwards, age 19, with second-degree murder, even though her body was nowhere to be found. Photo courtesy of The Gateway, University of Nebraska at Omaha's student newspaper.

Chapter 13

With Edwards locked away in a steel cage at the county jail, Dave Kofoed could roll back his comfy office chair, kick up his feet on his desk, and admire his own greatness.

The steam was starting to come out of the engines as the wheels of Nebraska's criminal justice system were starting to roll. The Edwards case was in the process of becoming Kofoed's shining accomplishment, the greatest professional triumph of his Nebraska law enforcement career.

For the time being, the June arrest of Edwards gave Kofoed a chance to come up for air and enjoy a quick breather. Without his incredible foresight on so many instances, the arrest of Edwards would not have happened.

He had picked through a garbage bag and out popped two bloody bath towels. He had the sneaking suspicion to recheck the suspect's trunk and only then did he find blood stains that his master's degree-level forensic scientists, Christine Gabig and Josh Connelly, both failed to spot on successive prior days. And Kofoed was front and center, calling the shots, when the sword was found in the basement and two sections of ceiling were sawed out of the basement bedroom.

If there was a highlight reel for CSI work, Kofoed's recovery of several previously hidden and painted-over blood stains concealed on the suspect's ceiling were worthy of making the tape. He also put himself in charge of finding the blood stains on the defendant's headboard. He reported finding at least fourteen different splotches.

All of this blood later proved to belong to Jessica.

Kofoed's self-confidence was on the uptick.

More than any other public theater, Kofoed thrived on the courtroom witness stand. He was a gifted oral communicator. He was highly persuasive. He loved to talk and ramble on about his CSI work. He was also in good graces with the lawyers in the Douglas County Attorney's Office, and they made him feel extra special.

The chief criminal prosecutor, Leigh Ann Retelsdorf, was an up-and-coming and highly ambitious lawyer. She was a stellar prosecutor in the courtroom who had loftier aspirations. She occasionally served as a featured public speaker at large police banquets and luncheons. She would later go on to become a Douglas County District Court judge. And it didn't hurt that she was also the older sister of one of

Kofoed's favorite members of his CSI team, forensic scientist CL Retelsdorf.

Leigh Ann would be tasked with trying to win the first jury trial in Nebraska involving a murder case without the recovery of the victim's body.

However, her younger brother's commander commonly delivered air-tight, slam-dunk cases for Douglas County criminal prosecutors, notably in high-profile murder cases that captured the city's spotlight. With Dave Kofoed as her star witness, Leigh Ann would have nothing to sweat when it came to prosecuting Jessica's despicable heartless boyfriend.

One of the bonuses of being in good graces with the prosecutor's office was that Kofoed's evidence harvests were all taken for granted as gospel.

Among others, Leigh Ann was not peppering her brother's boss with nagging, tough or uncomfortable questions surrounding many of his crime lab's forensic clues that seemed like they were rolling off an assembly line. Perhaps the enthusiasm and ravings from her much younger naïve brother blinded Leigh Ann.

Since Leigh Ann already had a positive working relationship with Kofoed, she, like the others in Douglas County's criminal justice system, blindly came to rely upon his clues and forensic evidence as being authentic and infallible rather than as kryptonite. Like her brother, she, too, fell victim to the Kofoed charade. She did not have the foggiest idea that she, too, was likely on his list of easy suckers.

As the Edwards case moved closer to trial, Kofoed was a key figure in the strategy exercised by the Douglas County Attorney's Office. After all, this was a rare case resting on the strength of the forensics and DNA clues. The work of the county crime lab made the arrest possible, now it was up to Kofoed and his unit to carry the ball over the goal line. He and the prosecutors were under an intense public spotlight to bring the reeling family and friends of Jessica O'Grady a conviction.

Kofoed would not have wanted it to any other way. He was a warrior in the courtroom. He was always prepared for the task.

During trial preparation, Kofoed collaborated with the prosecutor's office on the recruitment of various national blood-stain experts. They would be flown into Omaha on the taxpayer's expense to offer expert testimony for the prosecution.

One of the blood-stain celebrities was Stuart James of Fort Lauderdale, Florida. Several months before the trial, James traveled to Omaha to huddle with Kofoed and the prosecutor's office. James was provided a CSI video showing the macabre scene within the Edwards home. He reviewed a disk with gruesome images of the downstairs including the bloody mattress. He also studied the crime lab reports assembled by Kofoed's outfit.

To this day, one obscure clue from the Edwards case

still has James scratching his head. The hedge shears was one of the unusual and unexplainable objects that caught Kofoed's eye and became his preoccupation during the early days of the case.

Kofoed had the shears tested once at the University of Nebraska Medical Center Human DNA lab to no avail. Then, he brought them back to his crime lab. He waited a couple days. He then assigned employee Michelle Steele Potter to test them a second time. Afterward, Kofoed took it upon himself to gather up the new set of test specimens. He drove them back to the University of Nebraska Medical Center DNA. Next, he waited for the lab's final analysis.

On June 20, 2006, eleven days after Edwards was arrested for murder, the Nebraska Medical Center issued its preliminary DNA report back to Kofoed.

A number of clues matched the DNA of Jessica or Edwards.

Full DNA profiles of Jessica matched the west wall, south wall, and ceiling of Edwards's bedroom, his mattress, the blue towel, and his trunk. Additionally, Jessica's full DNA profiles were on the sword's handle and tip.

Her partial DNA profiles were reported on the lime green towel. Stunningly, her blood was allegedly found on the wooden handle of those pruning shears.

Kofoed's dogged determination to stay preoccupied with those garden clippers had paid off again. He had served up another boost for the prosecution. But how did the hedge shears factor into Jessica's murder? That was not so clear. As the case proceeded, the shears would fade into oblivion.

They would go down as another of those bizarre and confusing bloody clues of Kofoed's that did not seem to make any sense. The pruning shears did not seem at all relevant to Jessica's murder that certainly occurred in the basement bedroom of Edwards, and yet, they had sprung up like a poisonous mushroom anyway.

When internationally renowned blood-stain analyst Stuart James of Florida prepared his findings for Douglas County authorities, he validated the recovery of the blood on the hedge shears.

"Examination of the hedge shears recovered from the Honda Accord showed a black circled area on the right handle where a sample had been removed for testing," James stated. "The bloodstain on the right handle of the hedge shears from the Honda Accord matching the DNA of Jessica O'Grady is consistent with her blood having contact with that object."

Additionally, James had no information at that time to arouse suspicion or create room for doubt when it came to the blood stains in the trunk. "The bloodstain on the metal from the upper interior of the trunk matching the DNA of Jessica O'Grady is consistent with her blood having contact with that object," James noted.

In total, James deduced that Jessica's blood showed up on about a dozen different clues he was asked to review and analyze for the prosecution. James took the position that the Nebraska college coed met her untimely death by one of the ceremonial swords. Jessica died from at least seven separate overhead swings from the sword, he concluded. "The bloodstain on the Bangkok Battle sword matching the DNA of Jessica O'Grady is consistent with her blood having contact with that object," his report advised chief prosecutor Leigh Ann Retelsdorf.

Clearly, the suggestion that Edwards had killed Jessica with a souvenir Bangkok battle sword made the case incredibly memorable, James recalled. Other factors of the crime scene also stood out.

James said the ceiling evidence was clearly incriminating against Edwards. "You could easily see where it had been painted over, especially the portions of the ceiling where there had been the cast-off blood stains," James said. "There was no question in my mind that she was killed in the house in the basement, when you saw how much blood was on the mattress."

In preparation for trial, James remembered how Kofoed had produced a number of cuttings from the mattress and those sections were dissected. However, James said he simply could not give a definite answer as far as how much of Jessica's blood seeped into the mattress. He also could not tell whether Jessica was awake or asleep at the time of her slaughter.

As Edwards remained in jail facing murder charges, authorities and volunteers chased after any promising leads and tips that might lead to finding Jessica's body. That October, a team of all-terrain vehicles canvassed some open fields near 120th and Maple Streets. Weeks later, in November, a fire and rescue dive team was summoned to scour an Omaha neighborhood pond in a suburban housing development around 160th and Potter Streets. Both sites were in proximity to the Edwards property. Both search efforts were futile. The canvass of the fields and the dive team's submersion into water did not find any sign of Jessica's remains.

Jessica's family and the police grew more resigned to the grim possibility they might never find her, as long as Edwards was not confessing to the crime.

In fact, during the sixth month marking Jessica's tragedy, family and friends went ahead and held a memorial service. More than one hundred people mourned for Jessica's untimely loss at Omaha's St. Leo The Great Catholic Church near 102nd and Blondo Streets. That weekend, a short Jessica O'Grady obituary notice appeared in the Omaha newspaper. Jessica O'Grady, age 19, was survived by her mother, Rachelle (Shelly) O'Grady, her father Marc Fryer; grandparents Michael O'Grady, Sandie and Stoney Shotkoski; great grandparents Eduard and Martha Peter; brothers Eric Fryer, Andrew Winter and Dustin Winter; several aunts and uncles, numerous cousins; and two special faithful friends of hers, Kathryn (Kari) Peterson and Holly Stumme.

Lots of tear drops were shed that somber fall weekend.

"We can't forget that we were blessed for almost twenty years with Jessica's presence," her Aunt Shauna Stanzel told television station KETV.

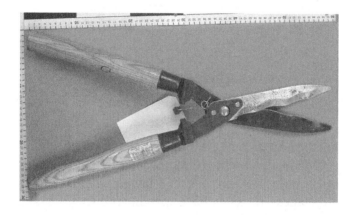

The pruning shears were a prime example of the kinds of unorthodox bloody clues that emerged with regularity from the Douglas County CSI lab during the period when Kofoed was planting blood. A tiny speck of Jessica's blood ultimately showed up on one wooden handle, yet none was present on the blades. This object was retrieved from the cluttered backseat of Edwards.

Chapter 14

In the American criminal justice system, every defendant deserves to be represented in the courtroom by a competent, professional lawyer. Defendants of all shapes and sizes have a right to due process as guaranteed by the U.S. Constitution.

At the end of the day, Christopher Edwards's parents agreed to retain a seasoned and experienced criminal defense lawyer by way of referral. Attorney Steve Lefler had worked with Matt Higgins, the Omaha divorce attorney who did legal work for Bob Edwards, the suspect's dad. However, Higgins knew he was out of his league when Chris Edwards was charged with murder. Higgins did not have expertise handling defense work in high-profile murder court cases.

After exchanging pleasantries, Lefler recalled how he and his new clients got off to an amicable start. Even though the parents were divorced, they both united and rallied on behalf on their son, who was in a perilous ordeal. The second-degree murder count carried a possible maximum of life imprisonment, and a minimum penalty of twenty years incarceration.

"They were one of the nicest families I've ever worked with," Lefler recalled. "The love they had for their child ... I can't say enough good things about the Edwards family."

Since the family was shelling out thousands of dollars to retain Lefler, they expected him to vigorously defend their son on second-degree murder charges. They desperately hoped he would poke holes in the prosecution's case.

Heading into the trial, Lefler believed he had a strong chance to prevail. A not-guilty verdict for his client was achievable. No medical doctor was willing to step forward to testify that Jessica O'Grady was dead just based on the photos of the blood-saturated mattress taken by the Douglas County Sheriff's Office, Lefler noted.

"I still think there has to be medical proof," Lefler explained. "In this case with no body, the state government could not present any testimony that the amount of blood on the mattress of that room necessarily resulted in death. No doctor would go there. It would have been different, had there been brains blown out, and there been pieces of brain matter scattered around on the floor, but there was none of that."

As the weeks rolled along, the well-known Omaha criminal defense lawyer immersed himself in the case. The case consumed his time.

"I dedicated my life to this case," Lefler said. "I would get up at 6 a.m. on Saturdays and Sundays and go into the office to work on it. And for several months before the trial, I even stopped taking on new cases. I read over the reports. I consulted with many experts. I was just very prepared for this particular case. I knew there was going to be bright lights in the courtroom, and I did not want to blink."

On the opposite side, chief Douglas County criminal prosecutor, Leigh Ann Retelsdorf was in charge of assembling her line-up of witnesses for the historic Nebraska murder trial. She penciled in Kofoed as her clean-up hitter. A large portion of the trial hinged on the preparation and presentation of the CSI commander. He would fulfill the role of foundation witness for the state.

* * *

By the time the trial began, the political winds of change had blown through the prosecutor's office in Omaha.

Former long-time chief deputy prosecutor, Donald Kleine, a Democrat, had staged a successful comeback victory in November of 2006. Kleine defeated Republican incumbent Stu Dornan, though Kleine's win was not unexpected.

Two months after Kleine took office in January of 2007, the hottest murder case in Omaha fell into his lap. When Edwards went on trial, Kleine gave himself a spot at the prosecutor's table, along with Leigh Ann Retelsdorf. As a result, two of the best prosecutors in

Nebraska would sit side by side, squaring off against Edwards and his criminal defense team led by Steve Lefler.

The Edwards murder case was sure to be the most hotly watched jury trial in the city of Omaha in quite a few years.

Days before the trial, Kofoed staged a unique made-for-media publicity stunt.

Stuart James, the Florida blood-stain analyst, came into town early to put on a week-long, blood-stain professional training seminar for several Douglas County prosecutors. Since Kofoed helped organize the event, he made sure the local news media was on hand to garner more notoriety for his thriving crime lab.

A story by *Omaha World-Herald* journalist Jason Kuiper detailed some of the bizarre and ghoulish aspects of the blood-spatter demonstration.

Kuiper reported how James drew his own blood and spit it out of his mouth for dramatic effects. Others played the persona of Vincent Price. They used deep, creepy voices to make the event entertaining for the news media. Kuiper's newspaper story, headlined "CSI: Omaha Science Reveals the Crime," featured comments from various national forensic experts visiting Omaha. They had only glowing things to say about Kofoed's forensics unit.

"People of this county should be damned proud. We travel all around, and these people are good," blood-spatter expert Todd Thorne of Kenosha, Wisconsin, said in the story.

Thorne singled out Kofoed's previous work on the Brendan Gonzalez murder case in Plattsmouth, Nebraska, from just a few years prior.

* * *

Heading into the trial, Steve Lefler sought to argue that someone other than his client harmed Jessica somewhere other than Christopher Edwards's bedroom.

Years later, Lefler recalled that Jessica was communicating with a guy in the military who lived in Texas. In addition, Jessica had had sexual encounters with others besides the defendant in the weeks prior to her disappearance, including with Christopher McClanathan, the convicted registered sex offender, the court records reflect.

In a noteworthy pretrial ruling, Douglas County District Judge J. Russell Derr scuttled the defense's idea of raising an alternative suspect defense. Edwards would not be cut any slack by this strict judge.

Without a doubt Lefler was treading on treacherous waters by taking the Edwards murder case to trial, remarked Omaha attorney William Gallup. Gallup has long been regarded as one of the elite criminal defense lawyers at the Douglas County Courthouse. A plea bargain to the reduced charge of felony manslaughter would have been a fair resolution for both the prosecution and defense, Gallup said. It was reasonable to infer that Jessica, age 19, was slain during the heat of passion or a sudden quarrel with her boyfriend of the same age, he added.

However, Edwards and his parents appeared to be hell bent on winning an acquittal at all costs, Gallup said. Edwards was not in favor of pleading guilty to any crime, regardless of leniency, at the time of sentencing.

Gallup said he would not have taken the Edwards case to trial as his defense lawyer. "It was an overwhelming case, a solid case for the state I thought," Gallup recalled. "If they're paying me, I tell people, 'It's my case, and I need to be in the driver's seat.' Here, I would have said, 'Look, you're not going to win this case. You do it my way or you get another lawyer.'

"I would have tried to negotiate a plea."

The Edwards case was destined for a jury trial, starting on March 21, 2007.

Chapter 15

Downtown Omaha is best known as a staple of major commerce and industry. It's anchored by Union Pacific railroad headquarters, ConAgra Foods, the First National Bank Tower, and Woodmen of the World insurance company.

During the last two weeks of March 2007, the fourth floor of a different downtown landmark, the 1912-era Douglas County Courthouse, captured the community's undivided attention.

The jury trial of State of Nebraska versus Christopher Edwards was officially underway. It took a few days to seat a jury. Many prospective jurists were sent packing after they admitted during jury selection process that their minds were already made up and Edwards was guilty. This was not a huge surprise. The general consensus around Omaha was Edwards should be found guilty.

Pretrial publicity was slanted exclusively in favor of the prosecution. During the previous ten months,

Sheriff Dunning and Kofoed took advantage of their cozy and tight relationship with the Omaha news media. Kofoed also gave one Omaha television station an exclusive a few months before Edwards went on trial. During an on-camera, blood-spatter demonstration using a dummy, Kofoed showed how Edwards may have caused the rampant blood spray within his room.

From Lefler's perspective, none of the pretrial publicity was improper, but it put him and his client at a tremendous disadvantage as they tried to seat an unbiased jury. Lefler later made the analogy of a beer company such as Budweiser that spends millions of dollars annually on television advertising "just to make sure you think about buying Budweiser when you go to the store. It's the same as getting a lot of media coverage in a case like this," Lefler reasoned. "Just like with Budweiser advertising, I think it impacts people subconsciously in an unknowing way. I think it has essentially the same impact on my client's chances to get a not-guilty verdict.

"All criminal cases are an uphill battle for a defense attorney," Lefler continued. "The cards are always stacked in the state's favor. Nobody has more time and money to take on a case like the state does. It's not a level playing field."

Even still, in a no-body murder case, the Omaha community did not take a murder conviction for granted. The trial was to take place in the fourth-floor courtroom of Douglas County District Judge J. Russell Derr. He had been appointed to the bench by the Nebraska governor back in 2003.

Tom Becka, one of Omaha's best-known media personalities, remembered that the Edwards trial became one of the most closely followed murder trials in the city in many years.

"There was a murder, a missing victim, sex, a girlfriend who had a baby with the defendant, and parents who would never admit their son might be guilty. It was a real-life made-for-TV cop show," said Becka, who provides nightly commentary on Omaha's Fox42 News.

The case was so huge that the *Omaha World-Herald*, Nebraska's largest newspaper, assigned several reporters to provide non-stop coverage during all two weeks of the trial. Reporters Todd Cooper, Lynn Safranek, and Christopher Burbach were all well-respected by their Omaha journalism peers as top-notch crime and court reporters.

Not to be outdone, Nebraska Education Television investigative journalist Bill Kelly provided in-depth daily blog updates during each day of the trial. Prior to the trial, Kelly had worked closely with Kofoed for an in-depth public television documentary that highlighted Nebraska CSI forensics work.

Once the trial got underway, the Douglas County prosecutors raved about the sheriff's CSI unit. CSI Christine Gabig testified how she found specks of blood on the tip of the blade of Edwards's sword. It was also revealed in court that the DNA of both the murder victim and the defendant were found on the sword's handle.

In Judge Derr's courtroom, Kofoed amazed the gallery with a sophisticated PowerPoint presentation that summarized the strong forensic evidence that had all piled up like a mountain against the murder defendant.

"We had a tremendous amount of trial preparation," Kofoed recalled. "Although it is common now, it was the first case in Douglas County that employed PowerPoint presentations, digitally projected images, 3D diagrams, and a 3D video recreation of the crime scene. We also presented three-foot-by-five-foot color-coded DNA charts and images from the scene to include the bloody mattress from the suspect's bedroom. It was a total team effort, but CSI played a major part of the investigation, trial preparation, and trial presentation."

As the face of the prosecution's case, Kofoed asserted on the witness stand how he identified numerous purported blood stains. This was the blood spatter the defendant tried to cover up with the white shoe polish Edwards bought at the Walgreens store a day after Jessica vanished.

Kofoed's appearance on the witness stand left the jury spellbound. Not surprisingly, NET investigative journalist Bill Kelly made this entry into his trial blog on March 23, 2007:

"Tall, bald and serious, Kofoed is well aware that how you present a case can be as important as what you present. He and every member of his team show

up in court in their para-military style CSI uniforms, shiny black boots, tailored pants and dark blue shirts with gold 'Crime Scene Investigator' embroidered on the back. The photos and diagrams of the crime scene are presented in the manner of a polished, high-tech PowerPoint. Kofoed draws attention to important details with his laser pointer."

Naturally, Kofoed downplayed any information that might cause jurors to grow skeptical or uneasy with his unit's performance. It worked to Kofoed's advantage that the jury presumed the authorities were all righteous and not nefarious. As far as the jury was concerned, the only villain was sitting at the defense table.

There was one mesmerizing exhibit that everyone in the courtroom anxiously anticipated. The prosecution showed large graphic images of the blood-soaked mattress that was hauled out of the defendant's basement bedroom.

"That photo of the blood was one of the most powerful pieces of evidence in my thirty-eight years as an attorney," Lefler recalled. "I've defended child-porn cases, and when juries see a film or a video of child porn and have to look away because they're just disgusted, I know we've lost the case. The mattress was similar in its effect. I could see by the look on the jury's faces, 'Oh, my God!'"

Lefler also knew there was no steering around the bloody mattress at trial. He had to tackle that ugly beast front and center.

In preparation for the trial, Lefler recalled how he and the murder defendant's father, Bob Edwards, went out and conducted various blood-stain experiments and tests using the blood of a dead pig. They tried to prove that the blood stains on the mattress might not have been deadly. Ultimately, their unconventional experiments with pig's blood were never presented in the courtroom at the jury trial.

"We bought three or four mattresses," Lefler explained. "There was more than one experiment, new versus old mattresses. We tried to replicate it. That's the kind of investigation we did."

The displaying of the mattress dominated the trial drama, but another riveting piece of evidence also enamored the media.

Obviously, a sensational murder trial demanded lots of shocking clues. The long sword fit the prosecution's narrative, so it became an important footnote in the trial that residents of Omaha would not soon forget.

At an opportune moment, Douglas County Attorney Don Kleine reached into a box strategically near his prosecution's table. For dramatic effect, Kleine displayed the nearly two-foot-long silver sword in the presence of the courtroom. The gallery contained about forty spectators. O'Grady's mother, Rachelle, gasped at the sight of the sword, the media reported.

"Alleged murder weapon creates a stir at trial," the next day's *Omaha World-Herald* newspaper headline read.

The defense, though, did not put forth a compelling challenge to the portrayal of the sword as the murder weapon, even though there was room to doubt its authenticity.

For instance, despite the massive bloodshed in Edwards's bedroom, the ceremonial battle sword only had invisible flakes of blood. The complete absence of blood stains was not developed as a theme by the defense. The credibility of the Douglas County Sheriff's Office CSI unit was not raised by defense lawyer Lefler.

Furthermore, Kofoed never had his feet held to the fire to explain why the probable murder weapon remained in his crime lab for nine days before it was finally analyzed. This period of uncanny apathy was going on during a time when Edwards remained free and had not been charged with killing Jessica.

"I do not remember all that much about the sword," Kofoed recalled years later. "I do not have anything to indicate the sword was the murder weapon or the hedge shears for that matter. I think that both were involved based on the evidence that was developed, but I would be guessing as to how both played into the case. The sword gained a lot of attention with the media."

One of Kofoed's former long-time crime lab employees, Darnel Kush, has a different recollection. She said Kofoed was enamored by the sword as part of the preparation for the Edwards trial.

"I remember Kofoed had asked another CSI to go

purchase a 'glass-framed shadow box' to display the sword for courtroom presentation," Kush said. "This struck me as odd. The sword was evidence, and I had never seen evidence packaged in this way. I heard from (Bill) Kaufhold that he was told by the prosecutor attorney to remove the sword from the shadow box."

* * *

As the trial moved along, one petite brunette caught the attention of the Omaha news media. Michelle Wilken was a nineteen-year-old aspiring beautician. She also had a baby girl named Macy. The infant was the lovechild of her and Edwards, the murder defendant on trial for killing his other girlfriend.

It remained to be seen how the jury and the press would react to her testimony. Would she throw Edwards to the lions or faithfully stand behind him at this pivotal moment, with his future at stake?

Chapter 16

Michelle Wilken's testimony was grotesque.

Michelle admitted in court she was ignorant about the blood-soaked mattress, just like she was clueless about her cheating and dangerous boyfriend.

The courtroom learned how Michelle and the murder defendant had indulged in more sexual intercourse within days of Jessica's murder on the very same bed that was drenched with Jessica's damp and moist blood stains, on the opposite side of the flipped mattress. The jury also heard how Michelle and Edwards had a heart-to-heart conversation just two days prior to Jessica's appearance about the prospect of marriage. Michelle later learned that Jessica was not satisfied with being an occasional one-night stand with Edwards. Michelle was under the impression that Edwards advised Jessica that he was definitely not interested in a serious long-term romance with Jessica.

"He said (Jessica) wanted more than just the time they

slept together, and she was trying for more than that, and he was telling her it wasn't going to happen," Michelle Wilken testified, according to Burbach's newspaper story.

On Jessica's last night alive, at approximately 12:20 a.m., she fired off that fateful text message to one of her best friends remarking, "No shenanigans (tonight) for Jessica."

Less than forty minutes later, at 12:58 a.m., Edwards had Michelle on his mind.

He sent her a message of warmth and comfort. "I love you. Good night," he text-messaged her.

Shortly thereafter, Jessica's blood was about to become drenched on the mattress, walls, headboard, and ceiling tiles across his bedroom.

It was obvious Jessica's murder happened silently during the night. Edwards's fourteen-year-old cousin and his Aunt Jane would testify during the trial that neither of them heard any loud noises, screams, or shrieks.

The next night, May 11, Michelle testified, she did not notice any blood spatter within her lover's bedroom, when she stopped over to see him.

Prosecutor Don Kleine asked if she saw the blood-soaked mattress.

"No," Michelle testified.

It was clear to courtroom observers that Michelle

was still endeared to Chris Edwards. When defense lawyer Steve Lefler got a chance to ask her questions, she was able to loosen up.

"Are you still talking about getting married?" Lefler asked her.

"Yes," Michelle answered proudly.

For one of the only moments during the trial, Edwards felt good. His gullible and petite princess gave him a tiny glimmer of hope. If Michelle Wilken was still in the defendant's corner, perhaps the jury might be, as well.

The March 28, 2007, Omaha newspaper headline was right on the money: *"Girlfriend loyal on the stand: She says she and murder suspect still hope to marry."*

* * *

As expected, the bloody mattress and the Bangkok battle sword made an impression on jurors, but Douglas County Attorney Don Kleine urged the jury to focus on something else.

Kleine hammered home his belief the blood stains from the trunk were of even greater magnitude.

"I think it's very significant when we talk about the blood that appeared in the defendant's car," Kleine reminded the jury. "Remember that? You see, there's a picture of Dave Kofoed from the Douglas County Sheriff's Office. He's inside the trunk of that vehicle, and he's looking up underneath the trunk on the inside portion. That's where this piece of metal comes from."

The blood in the trunk cemented the prosecution's theory that the defendant's car was used to dispose of Jessica somewhere unknown. "And what did the gasket between those two red rubber bands have on it?" Kleine asked rhetorically. "It was Jessica O'Grady's blood in the trunk of Christopher Edwards's motor vehicle. How do you think, how did that get there?"

Between the bloodshed in the bedroom and everything extra Kofoed produced to bring the prosecutor's office an infallible case, the defendant's prospects of winning an acquittal looked dismal, even in a no-body case.

Besides, Edwards did not help matters by making a half-hearted effort to clean up the blood rampant in his bedroom, as the prosecutor duly noted. "You've seen the feeble attempts by the defendant to clean up," Kleine reminded jurors. "You've seen not only the blood that appeared in this trunk, but the blood on these towels.

"And again the most important piece, I believe, is the trunk of that car."

Without Jessica's body and no eyewitnesses, the murder trial hinged on the strength of the prosecution's circumstantial evidence.

* * *

In a tactical blunder, Lefler made the decision to go easy on the prosecution's primary witness. Kofoed claimed during his trial testimony that CSI Josh Connelly merely conducted a walk around of Edwards's dark Honda before Kofoed returned the next morning to find the blood stains in the trunk.

Lefler also whiffed on the chance to make Kofoed justify why he took it upon himself to fill out the forensic report of Connelly's unsuccessful search of the Edwards car. Generally speaking, the CSIs filled out their own reports, and not the boss. However, the narrative CSI report of the car's initial processing shows it was both written and approved by Kofoed. Moreover, Lefler did not focus on why the supposed weapon sat in the evidence unit under Kofoed's direct control for nine days before it was finally processed? Or why a lone speck was left on the tip of the blade, but no visible blood stains were present in the mesh sheaths that were holding the sword in place?

When the trial mattered most, when it came time to cross examine Kofoed, Lefler chose not to act like a tenacious bulldog or a mighty lion. Instead, the defense lawyer purred like a little kitten.

Their courtroom exchanges were reminiscent of two old fraternity brothers bellying up to the bar for a round of drinks.

"Dave, I always feel awkward interviewing you, cross-examining you, because we've become friends," Lefler told Kofoed in the courtroom.

* * *

Most of the gallery seated in Judge Derr's courtroom during the agonizing, two-week trial, came to support Jessica. Her family and friends were ardent backers of the masterful work turned in by the Douglas County Sheriff's Office and Kofoed. Speaking of the ace commander: toward the tail end of the trial, he strutted into the courtroom at a most convenient moment. He, along with Sheriff Tim Dunning, came to watch the expert witness testimony of Stuart James, the blood-stain analyst from Florida. James remembered how Edwards was quite stoic at the defense table during the trial. "He just sat there. He didn't react emotionally," James said.

Clearly, the suggestion that Edwards had killed Jessica with a souvenir Bangkok battle sword made the trial a case James and others would never forget.

James has testified in a handful of murder cases over the years that involved swords, but those slayings typically involved machetes. The sword portrayed as the weapon that killed Jessica can be purchased online through a karate or martial arts website.

When asked later why there was only a bit of blood on the sword, given the fact that Edwards's mattress was a bloodbath, James said it was possible Edwards "cleaned off the sword but not enough of it," thus leaving behind the scant traces of blood and DNA that later connected back to him and Jessica.

"It did have a sharp point," James clarified. "That's a lethal weapon."

* * *

As the trial wound down, Lefler chose not to put his client on the witness stand.

And he also chose to put forth an unbelievably outrageous defense to fight for an innocent verdict for his client.

Douglas County Attorney Don Kleine urged the Omaha jury deciding the fate of Edwards to focus on the blood stains that CSI commander Dave Kofoed found in the defendant's trunk.

Chapter 17

Lefler claimed the large pool of blood that saturated his client's mattress came from Edwards and Jessica engaging in wild sex while she was in the full-blown stages of her menstrual cycle.

"If Chris is a peaceful kid, might there be some other explanations?" Lefler pondered. "What else happens when a woman discharges in the bed? I hate saying this with the press and everyone here, but has anyone used sex toys before? Has anyone ever done it doggy style? Use your judgment based on what happened in your life."

Sheriff Dunning grew incensed by Lefler's arguments, shaking his head in disbelief, the media reported.

"I don't know what happened," Lefler continued. "Miscarriage? Abortion? Sex game-gone wrong?

"Is it just as likely that Jessica O'Grady started a new life for herself?"

Lefler pointed out that Jessica had recently purchased airline tickets to visit a man in San Antonio just weeks before she vanished from Omaha. "Jessica was talking to this guy down in San Antonio," Lefler offered. "People disappear and then years later, show up."

The jury was informed that dozens of searches across the wilderness and other parts of eastern Nebraska all failed to find Jessica's remains.

"They say (Edwards) took this shovel and buried her," Lefler argued. "My contention is that this is not Jessica O'Grady's blood, or at least they have not proven it to a reasonable doubt."

Lastly, Lefler urged the jury to find his client not guilty. No body, no murder, he argued. It was as if the defense desperately hoped the jury should penalize the prosecution because Edwards successfully got rid of Jessica's body.

"If I have done something to offend you, please don't take it out on my client," Lefler concluded.

* * *

Jill Melancon and Jessica O'Grady both had been students at the University of Nebraska at Omaha campus. In 2007, Melancon never fathomed she would be picked for the jury to determine the guilt or innocence of Christopher Edwards.

"The crime scene was Jessica telling us something awful had happened to her," Melancon told her student paper, the *Gateway*, after the trial. "This was no accident."

On March 31, 2007, the jury took about eleven hours to reach its unanimous verdict. "There wasn't a single female juror that had dry eyes," Melancon told the *Gateway*. "We all started crying."

Melancon was one of eleven original jurors to agree from the outset that Edwards deserved to be convicted of second-degree murder. But one woman on the jury was not immediately convinced beyond a reasonable doubt. She was in favor of the lesser felony, manslaughter. Inevitably, the other eleven jurors persuaded the lone hold-out to change her mind during deliberations, the *Gateway* reported.

Besides second-degree murder, Edwards was also found guilty of use of a deadly weapon.

The Edwards verdict was historic for Nebraska. It marked the first time a defendant was successfully prosecuted in a no-body murder trial.

"A jury convicted Edwards of slashing O'Grady, 19, with a sword in an attack so brutal that her blood sprayed his ceiling, two walls of his room and a TV ten feet away, and formed a pool on an eight-square-foot section of his mattress. He then hid her body," the *Omaha World-Herald* newspaper reported.

Tom Becka, the Omaha radio and television personality, said Edwards was destined for a guilty verdict no matter what.

"I'm not sure if he had gotten rid of the mattress it would have mattered," Becka said. "From what I've heard, when they tested the room with Luminol, it showed blood all over the room. I'll also play pop psychologist here and say that I don't believe anyone who ever breaks the law, whether it be speeding or murder actually thinks they will ever get caught. So I'm sure he felt the bloody mattress would never be discovered, so he was in the clear."

In retrospect, Lefler's trial tactics were more harmful than helpful, noted Gallup, the prominent Omaha defense lawyer who closely followed the case.

"Lefler is a good attorney," Gallup said. "But some of the arguments seemed not to make any sense. To suggest the blood was from a menstrual period was so out of line. It was an offensively ludicrous argument. But, a lawyer has to do what he can for his client. It was a fairly difficult situation to sell to a jury when your client wants an all-or-nothing case."

Lefler said the trial hinged on the lack of cell phone communication between Jessica and Edwards after the night of May 10, 2006.

Testimony showed that Jessica never used her cell phone again after making her last phone call to Edwards while driving to his home nearing midnight. Prosecutors proved Edwards never tried to call Jessica after May 10 because he knew he already killed her.

"I'm still bleeding in that I lost the case. But I'm proud of the work that I put into it," Lefler said.

* * *

Trial testimony revealed Jessica's last communication before her brutal death was the text she sent to her long-time friend Kari Peterson.

With Edwards on the verge of being sentenced, Peterson penned a well-crafted letter. She informed the court of the best friend who brought joy into the world, whose murder now left everyone with sorrow and nagging questions.

Peterson's letter was presented to Judge Derr to consider at the June 15 sentencing.

She and Jessica first met as freshmen students at Westside High School. Their friendship lasted through good times and rocky ones. Out of nowhere, everything came to a screeching halt on May 10, 2006.

"Christopher Edwards not only took her life, but he took a part of my life and many others with it," Peterson wrote.

"I remember the first and only time I met him. This was not an 'I told you so situation' because he did not raise red flags for me. It just shows how much any person is capable of. He had met her friends and roommates and knowing how much they all meant to her still had the nerve to commit such a ghastly crime."

Peterson and Jessica had talked about their dreams and future. Jessica expressed interest in going to hair design school. Peterson told the court she would have supported Jessica in that endeavor. "We have become friends through many years and many hard times. Whether it was the movies, my house for lunch between classes, her house to make shirts for spirit week, or family gatherings, we did it all together. This was until May 10, 2006."

Peterson urged the judge to send Edwards to prison for the rest of his life. His lack of remorse was appalling. "I do not have a grave to visit or somewhere to put flowers for her birthday or go to just be with her and talk to her," Peterson wrote the judge. "There is nothing. And that is because of Christopher Edwards, he has made the decision to leave the family at this midway point."

* * *

Courthouse security was tight as the shackled prisoner was led back into the fourth floor courtroom of Judge Derr for his final proceeding, on June 15, 2007.

Edwards, age 20, faced a prison sentence ranging from twenty years to life. It was anybody's guess what the judge would decide. Perhaps Edwards was ready to unleash the most intimate details of the gory crime, now that his fate was sealed and a severe prison term was inevitable. Besides, a full admission of guilt and a deep sense of remorse might cause the judge to take notice.

In a most bizarre courtroom statement, Bob Edwards, the murder defendant's father, chose to address the courtroom, on behalf of his convicted son, who sat at the defense table nearby.

"Good afternoon, your honor. I'll be brief," Bob Edwards said.

"Take all the time you want," Derr replied.

Bob Edwards began by pointing out that "Mr. Kleine did a good job convincing the jury that Christopher is guilty, although the jury probably didn't need that much convincing from the start."

The killer's father reminded the judge that numerous letters had been submitted to the court on behalf of his son. "I trust you've read the letters from our family and friends, people who've known Christopher his entire life, attesting to his gentle demeanor, strong moral character, Christian upbringing, spotless record," Mr. Edwards testified.

Bob Edwards advised the courtroom that his son was offered plea deals on numerous occasions prior to the trial in exchange for revealing Jessica's whereabouts. "Christopher would have accepted the plea deal if he could," Bob Edwards told the judge. "But, honestly, he had no choice. He honestly does not know where she is.

"Perhaps Mr. Kleine would be better served asking that question to the three suspects that Mr. Dunning chose not to investigate: two boyfriends, one with a violent history, the other who was a registered sex offender, and a third man who flew in from Texas on May 9th of last year to meet Ms. O'Grady and then left Omaha for eastern Iowa on the night of May 10th."

Next, Mr. Edwards made an announcement that stunned the onlookers and members of the press.

"There's not a member of our family who doesn't pray daily for Ms. O'Grady to be guided back to her family alive and well," he began. "Finding Ms. O'Grady is becoming our last hope to prove Christopher's innocence. Therefore, we'll match the $10,000 reward being offered to finding her, with the stipulation that none of that money would go to (sheriff) Dunning or his crew. Christopher continues to be punished in many more ways than being locked in a jail cell."

Shauna Stanzel, Jessica's aunt who raised her, was profoundly amazed at how the Edwards family continued to live in total denial. She also had a chance to address the packed courtroom prior the sentencing pronouncement.

"No one wants to believe that Jessica's friend, Chris Edwards, one that she trusted, invited her over to his house, viciously killed her with a sword, and then dumped her body," Stanzel testified. "But that is exactly what the evidence has proven. And an objective group of people, a jury of his peers selected and approved by him and his defense team, have decided."

Jessica's murder was brutal. There was no hint she

fought back. "She had no options and no weapon to defend herself or the developing embryo that she carried," Stanzel pleaded. "It may have been difficult to continue hiding the infidelity that plagued his relationship with Michelle if another girl showed evidence of that unfaithfulness. Whatever his motives were, he was not justified in what he did. And these were not the actions of a peaceful person."

Lastly, Judge Derr turned to the defendant, Chris Edwards.

"Mr. Edwards, is there anything you'd like to tell me?" the judge inquired.

"I will respectfully decline, your honor," Jessica's killer responded.

Edwards chose to stand silent at his sentencing hearing. The young man who had carried a Bible with his name etched on the front cover in his car continued to cherish and hold on to his mortal sin: thou shall not kill.

"All right, very good," Derr advised.

On that somber summer day in the Douglas County Courthouse, the judge determined a severe sentence was in order.

"I have tried not to imagine the details of what happened in that bedroom on that day in May of 2006," Derr told the defendant. "Whatever happened had to be horrific. Ms. O'Grady's fear and likely suffering as she died is inconceivable."

153

Edwards did not receive the maximum penalty of life in prison without parole. The judge took into consideration that a number of other second-degree murder convictions handled by his fellow Douglas County judges did not result in life terms. As a result, Derr imposed a punishment totaling one hundred years imprisonment.

The defendant got eighty years for second-degree murder and another twenty years for the felony weapon conviction. Edwards was given credit for 372 days of jail time already served.

"This means, under the truth-in sentencing law, sir, that your first eligible for parole will be (in) fifty years, less the days you've already served," Derr advised.

The twenty-year-old Nebraskan would be housed in a maximum security prison nestled outside the small southeastern Nebraska farming community of Tecumseh, an hour's drive from both Omaha and Lincoln.

He would spend his days and nights at Nebraska's most dangerous prison facility. The worst of the worst ended up at Tecumseh, often lifers. Edwards was destined to be remembered as one of Omaha's most inhumane killers.

"When I first viewed Chris Edwards, he seemed small and frail looking," Kofoed recalled. "He reminded me of Ivan Henk in build and stature. As you know, Henk had murdered his small son about three years previously."

The public's portrayal of Edwards as a bloodthirsty premeditated monster was a contrast to the young man his defense lawyer saw —an average teenager.

"I enjoyed working with him," Lefler later said. "He's a great kid. I liked him a lot. He was found guilty of murder. All the while I was working with him, just based on his personality and how he treated me, he was a polite, smart, young kid. I never thought he would be capable of doing something like this."

* * *

If Chris Edwards had taken accountability for his actions – and taken control of his own defense – he would have received a prison sentence far, far, less than one hundred years.

"From the beginning, the father was telling everybody that they are not going to convict him without the body," recalled James Martin Davis, the family's original criminal lawyer, whom they fired.

Davis said he explained to the Edwards family that the absence of Jessica's body would make no difference to a jury, and given the set of facts, it would probably be more damaging to Chris' defense.

"Talking to the dad was like trying to blow out a light bulb," Davis said. "When evidence is circumstantial and very strong, dots are laid out and the jury will connect those dots on their own. I explained that to dad."

If Chris Edwards had accepted the plea deal that

Davis brokered, he was guaranteed at being released from prison no later than the summer of 2016, just shy of his thirtieth birthday.

"If Chris would have disclosed where the body was and pled guilty to manslaughter, the most he would have got was twenty years (minimum) to twenty years (maximum)," Davis said. "At most, he would have jammed out of prison after ten years. If he would have gotten a sentence of ten to twenty years, he could have been paroled in five years, so he would be out by now, but his father was calling the shots. Chris was only nineteen at the time. By rejecting my advice, the son winds up getting a life sentence (more or less). It was not in their best interest to go to trial."

* * *

Overall, Omaha cheered the Edwards prison sentence. Still, the city and the victim's family longed for more answers. Everyone wanted to know the real events that took place in Edwards's bedroom after dark on May 10-11, 2006.

But Edwards chose to haunt and taunt Omaha by his intentional silence. With his lips sealed, he held the deck of cards. He controlled the knowledge surrounding Jessica's cruel fate. And, as time marched on, Edwards continued to thumb his nose at the Nebraska news media. Some killers like to boast of their murders. Others like to justify their actions.

Edwards was a far different breed. He staunchly refused to grant any media interviews. He wanted to keep the intimate details of this heinous and tragic murder a deep, dark secret.

As for Kofoed, the Edwards trial marked the pinnacle accomplishment of his law enforcement career. People who followed the trial would never forget his heroics and magical feats. People around Omaha felt Kofoed deserved a debt of gratitude. He brought the friends and family of Jessica O'Grady justice inside the courtroom.

His clues cemented the murder defendant's fate at trial. His comrades at the sheriff's office and the Douglas County Attorney Office exalted his performance.

After the Edwards trial, Dave Kofoed was well on his way to building his own empire at the Douglas County Sheriff's Office. In fact, he could have been on his way to having a county government building named in his honor, which was a common way for Nebraska politicians to honor their distinguished leaders.

Architectural plans were underway to expand his county crime lab's capabilities. The old county veteran's home building, near the sheriff's office, was designated as the preferred site for a new high-tech Douglas County crime lab. It would not take much arm twisting on behalf of Sheriff Tim Dunning to move ahead with building plans. The sheriff's office had at least $4 million squirreled away in a drug forfeiture slush fund that was burning a hole in the agency's pocket.

The sheriff and Kofoed desired a state-of-the-art

forensic crime laboratory that would become the envy of Nebraska's law enforcement agencies. The Edwards trial served as the perfect prop to showcase the lab's outstanding work.

Years later, Kofoed was asked to reflect on whether he deserved all the credit for ensuring Edwards was found guilty of murder.

"Me personally?" Kofoed said. "Heck no! The folks that worked around me day in and day out are well aware that it was always about the team. We had a very, very good team, and Jessica O'Grady deserved our best effort."

Back in 2007, the crime lab commander's popularity had skyrocketed to new heights, but like a helium balloon, that gas would eventually seep out. He would never again soar so high in Nebraska's law enforcement community.

"My career and in some ways my life was ultimately shattered because of some very basic human faults directed at both me and some very good folks at CSI," Kofoed explained years later. "Human traits as simple as personal animosity, envy, and professional jealousy attacked a very good organization."

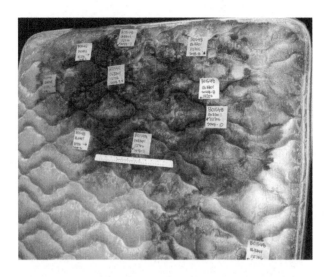

Omaha criminal defense attorney Steve Lefler told the jury that perhaps the defendant's mattress was drenched with Jessica's blood because of a sex-game gone wrong while she was in her menstrual cycle.

In 2007, Edwards, age 20, became the first Nebraska defendant convicted in a no-body murder trial. Edwards did not take the witness stand in his own defense. Photo courtesy of The Gateway, University of Nebraska at Omaha's student newspaper.

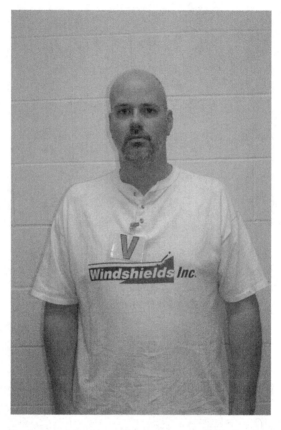

In a highly unusual move, Bob Edwards, father of the murder defendant, addressed the court on behalf of his adult son at the sentencing hearing. "I pray your final decision is logical, thoughtful and unbiased," Bob Edwards concluded in his remarks before Judge J. Russell Derr.

Chapter 18

For many years, Greater Omaha took a hear-no-evil, see-no-evil approach on touchy matters such as public corruption by so-called public servants. But don't kid yourself. On a per capita basis, the Omaha metro area tended to have as much political graft and misconduct as other major cities.

In recent history, there have been countless examples of Nebraska public officials and elected leaders engaging in abuse of power or shameful behavior that led to their ouster from public life.

In 2007, an Omaha Police officer was found guilty of sexual assault after forcing a street prostitute to provide him oral sex in his squad car. The officer faced up to fifty years in prison, but the judge instead put him on probation for five years.

In 2009, an aspiring suburban Omaha Republican mayor and attorney suddenly resigned from public office. Despite knowing the details, others at the Papillion City Hall stayed quiet about the facts of his stunning departure. Some city officials even hoped he could revive his political career perhaps a short while later. Then, a few months later, the dam burst and the facts finally came out. The former mayor had been involved in an office romance with his blonde-haired executive assistant, and she also got a staggering bump in pay. Then came a fallout when the secretary accused the mayor of sexual harassment. The City of Papillion ultimately paid her about $225,000 to resolve her claim before she ever filed a lawsuit. In addition, the city insisted to its insurance carrier that the settlement agreement should not be regarded as a public record, in the hopes of keeping it a secret. The growing suburb was incredibly sensitive toward negative publicity in the press.

In 2012, the veteran police chief of Nebraska's third-largest city, Bellevue, resigned in disgrace after the press reported he had a relationship with a female city administrator in nearby Gretna. Her own share of problems led to her termination from Gretna City Hall where she misused several thousand dollars of her own city's funds for personal use, including outlet mall shopping sprees and the purchase of lingerie, a state audit determined. Furthermore, she and the Bellevue police chief had attended several national government conferences together, which gave them the chance to rendezvous. The police chief's ultimate downfall was giving the divorced woman an unregistered handgun to keep at her suburban house for protection. The whole drama made for front-page newspaper stories over many months. The woman wound up pleading guilty to several misdemeanor charges of theft and was hauled off to jail.

When the police chief resigned his position, residents were outraged to later learn he had fleeced his taxpayers. Over the years, he had amassed a staggering stockpile of unused vacation days. The outgoing chief, in his mid-fifties, was paid more than $196,000 for his unused vacation bank, in addition to his normal police pension for his many years of public service for the City of Bellevue that stretched back to the late 1970s.

And, yet all of these disgraceful exits by Omaha area public officials were small potatoes compared to the scandalous storm brewing at the Douglas County Sheriff's Office between 2008 and 2010.

Of course, like most bad tornadoes, residents of Omaha and leaders of the Douglas County Sheriff's Office were caught off-guard; Dave Kofoed, a powerful and mighty Nebraska public figure, was working on the dark side of law enforcement and doing so for some time.

* * *

By the spring of 2008, the Omaha branch of the FBI had launched a top-secret police misconduct probe surrounding the Murdock farmhouse killings in neighboring Cass County. That was the double murder case that happened in April 2006, only three weeks before Jessica O'Grady's disappearance in Omaha. In the Murdock case, Kofoed claimed to find a speck of blood in a tan, four-door Ford Contour during a questionable follow-up search. This was the purported getaway car for a pair of Nebraska cousins pegged by the local cops as the apparent killers. The first search of the car under Kofoed's oversight came up empty. Then, he returned to the car at his agency's impound lot, a week later and found a speck of blood.

Kofoed's find kept the two cousins in jail for months, despite no evidence at the scene of the bloody crime linking back to them.

Inevitably, the forensic evidence steered the cops to two different people. Matt Livers and Nick Sampson were innocent. The farmhouse killers were from Wisconsin, a pair of teenage spree killers, who stole a truck in their native state to drive across the Midwest. Kofoed had planted blood against two innocent people because he took the local cops' word for it that the cousins were guilty. Despite realizing his blunder, Kofoed chose to stay silent. Months later, the local prosecutor freed the wrongly accused men from jail, and the real killers pleaded guilty.

The FBI later took it upon itself to flush out how the blood of a murder victim ended up in the wrong getaway car. And its suspicions led to Kofoed, since he was the one who found it. The FBI started to wonder: Did Kofoed really plant the evidence? The mighty CSI commander was showing chinks in his armor.

With a full-blown FBI investigation underway, Kofoed knew his career in law enforcement was in jeopardy. His image was endangered. The credibility of the Douglas County CSI unit he built was coming under question. He needed an attorney to go to bat for him. Someone he could trust. A good friend.

Sure enough, one Omaha criminal defense attorney stepped up on the CSI commander's behalf. This lawyer would mount a vigorous defense.

Steve Lefler was back in the news, again.

* * *

In March 2009, Kofoed went against the advice of Lefler and chose to testify before a federal grand jury probing his role in handling evidence in the Murdock murder case. On April 29, he was indicted by the U.S. Attorney's Office. On the day of the indictment's unsealing, Kofoed found out that a special prosecutor had filed a separate felony count accusing Kofoed of tampering with evidence. That charge was filed in state court in Cass County.

Kofoed had two separate criminal battles ahead. Sheriff Dunning stood by Kofoed, letting him stay on paid administrative leave. The tarnished CSI leader was allowed to remain free, pending trial. By August, he was standing trial in the U.S. District Court in downtown Omaha facing four federal charges. Two counts of civil rights violations, mail fraud, and falsifying public records.

Those charges accused Kofoed of intentionally falsifying his CSI report and failing to properly log the bloody filter paper into evidence. The federal prosecutors chose to sidestep the more sinister allegations of blood planting or manufacturing clues.

165

As a result, the prosecution's case was confusing and hard for the jury to understand.

On September 10, 2009, the jury needed less than an hour to reach a unanimous verdict. It found Kofoed not guilty on all counts. His lawyer Steve Lefler prevailed and scored a huge victory.

But the celebration was short lived. The evidence tampering trial in state court would be a totally different kind of case.

* * *

In March of 2010, a respected and long-time judge in neighboring Cass County, Randall Rehmeier, heard evidence presented by special prosecutor Clarence Mock related to two separate murder cases from Cass County. In both cases, Kofoed was suspected of planting the blood of victims to bolster the prosecution's case.

One case was the 2003 murder of little Brendan Gonzalez of Plattsmouth. Brendan was slain by his monster of a father, Ivan Henk. The other was the 2006 Murdock farmhouse killings where Livers and Sampson, the pair of local cousins, had been wrongly held in jail for many months based on a botched probe at the Cass County Sheriff's Office in Plattsmouth.

The judge sized up the evidence. He studied both cases laboriously. The judge recognized the Douglas County Sheriff's Office counted on an acquittal. In fact, Sheriff Dunning even took the stand during the bench trial and testified in defense of Kofoed. The sheriff informed the court he hoped to reinstate

Kofoed as crime lab manager once the trial was over.

When the trial ended, Judge Randall Rehmeier found Kofoed guilty. On June 1, 2010, the righteous judge sentenced Kofoed to four years in prison. Kofoed had to serve two years before reaching his mandatory release date.

Sheriff Dunning was flabbergasted. The man he hired away from Omaha to run the county's crime lab turned out to be a criminal himself.

Reluctantly, the sheriff had to part ways with Kofoed. Once the conviction was entered, the county was notified to terminate the CSI director's pay. By that point, Kofoed received more than $70,000 while on administrative leave as his court case was pending.

Kofoed's shameful exit from Nebraska's law enforcement community was bad enough for Omaha to swallow. He disgraced himself and his profession. He gained infamy for being one of the few crime lab personnel ever found guilty in the criminal courts of planting blood evidence in major violent crimes.

Omaha residents were shaken. The very same CSI commander who brought them reassurance and was a regular presence on the local television news during the Edwards trial – was carted off to prison himself for being a crook.

Lawyers began to speculate he fabricated evidence in the Edwards case.

After all, Kofoed directed that murder investigation, too.

Chapter 19

As elected politicians, Douglas County Attorney Don Kleine and Sheriff Tim Dunning were not in favor of conducting an outside independent probe surrounding Kofoed's work on the Edwards case.

The logical place to start was back at the sheriff's office where Kofoed was employed for more than ten years as lab supervisor.

"I don't remember any investigation being conducted by the sheriff's office regarding Kofoed and the Edwards case," county crime lab technician Darnel Kush said. "At that time, the administration and other CSI thought he was the forensic guru. It bothered me that my coworkers, investigators, and outside agencies did not question Kofoed. Other investigators did not work as close with Kofoed as I did. However, I was always baffled why nobody could see what I was seeing."

By 2010, Kush became an outcast in her unit. It was revealed during Kofoed's 2010 bench trial that she had served as a confidential informant for the FBI. She helped them build their corruption case against her boss. Kush had long suspected he was dirty and might even be planting fingerprints in various cases to make it appear he found evidence others missed.

Some of Kofoed's employees took the news of his felony conviction hard. His former captain, Dean Olson, attended Kofoed's sentencing and later made trips to Lincoln to visit Kofoed as he served out his prison term. CSI Christine Gabig also remained in contact with Kofoed while he was in prison.

Kush, now retired from the crime lab, had long suspected that Kofoed's role in tampering with blood in the two Cass County murder cases was just the tip of the iceberg.

"After all came to light, I was curious why the Douglas County Attorney's Office did not contact me," Kush said. "I am not sure why but my personal opinion is they did not want to hear anything because they would have to act, and they did not want any lawsuits."

The prevailing attitude at the sheriff's office was out of sight, out of mind. The sheriff advised the local press corps that Kofoed's conviction was an isolated incident. The sheriff maintained he had no knowledge Kofoed engaged in any other evidence planting schemes.

Although Sheriff Dunning and prosecutor Don Kleine were opposite political parties, both relied on each other to make it through the Kofoed scandal without being muddied themselves.

Foremost, the Kofoed fiasco needed to go away. The sheriff's agency did not need more bad press than the damage it encountered by virtue of Kofoed's historic bench trial. Likewise, Kleine did not need every judge and every criminal defense attorney banging on his office door, filing motion after motion, seeking a litany of new trials for every Omaha defendant under the sun. Dozens of convictions could be at stake if judges in Omaha opened the vaults and threw out every convict's case Kofoed had a stake in the final outcome, big or small.

Likewise, the Douglas County justice system was like a steamroller. It was a massive moving machine that was not designed to roll backward. The prosecutor's office and judges were already swamped with a long and never ending docket of murder trials and drug conspiracy cases. The hard-working and woefully underpaid assistant prosecutors were not enthused about the prospect of revisiting old cases. Consequently, the judges were in the same boat. The leading powerbrokers at the Douglas County Courthouse had a strong desire to keep the Kofoed can of worms from spilling into their courtrooms and squirming all over their floors.

The courthouse legal system hoped for the Kofoed scandal to fade away and become yesterday's old news.

Kofoed's name stopped being mentioned around Omaha's law enforcement and judicial circles.

He stood for so many bad memories. Sure, he had emerged as the star prosecution witness during the Edwards jury trial. But was any of his work legitimate?

Judge J. Russell Derr presided over the Edwards trial and put the killer where he belonged: in prison for a long time. But in light of Kofoed's extraordinary evidence tampering conviction by a neighboring county judge, the Edwards murder case was destined to be revisited.

The case was no longer about a missing murder victim and a jilted lover's triangle. It had transformed overnight into a case of legal precedence. Would power be preserved? Would legacies remain intact in Omaha, Nebraska? Would the Douglas County Sheriff's Office salvage the shared vision and dream of Sheriff Dunning and Kofoed to open a new top-of-the-line regional crime laboratory, a facility that might make the larger Omaha Police Department envious?

Judge Derr did not bat an eye. He knew community sympathy toward Edwards was virtually nonexistent in Omaha. And yet nagging questions persisted regarding the severity of Kofoed's forensic fraud on the Douglas County judicial system.

On the other hand, this was Omaha, not San Francisco or New York City, where the legal community was far more liberal and politically active. Nobody in Omaha was beating on a drum or staging giant protests outside the Douglas County Courthouse.

John Ferak

Citizens were not clamoring for new trials for any convicted killers whose cases passed through the dirty crime lab commander.

Chapter 20

There is no doubt Judge Derr did not want to let Christopher Edwards out of prison or be given a new trial even if strong circumstantial evidence showed Kofoed manufactured false clues against Edwards.

In short, any ruling against Jessica's killer marked a favorable ruling for Omaha's law enforcement community and prosecutor's office. The justice community wanted Kofoed's shameful actions put to rest.

While Kofoed was still serving time in prison in 2011, Judge Derr was asked to grant Edwards an evidentiary hearing. By now, there was a new lawyer hired to represent the Edwards family. Attorney Brian Munnelly wanted to present new evidence before the judge showing Kofoed tainted the jury trial by cobbling together a slew of clues that were never clues to begin with.

"In Edwards's bedroom, blood was purportedly found on the headboard, nightstand, clock radio and ceiling above the bed," Munnelly stated in his legal brief. "A large bloodstain was found on the underside of the mattress. Law enforcement claimed to have found blood on the handle of garden shears found in Edwards's vehicle. Law enforcement claimed that blood was found on the trunk gasket of the car and the underside of the trunk lid. At the end of the second search, a sword was found in Edwards's closet and a Douglas County CSI examiner claimed to have found blood that was later determined to match that of O'Grady.

"Douglas County CSI Commander David Kofoed was personally and extensively involved in both crime scene searches of Edwards's bedroom and vehicle and in the collection and processing of evidence collected."

Judge Derr rejected the lawyer's motion in convincing fashion.

The ruling made it easier for Sheriff Dunning to pick up the broken pieces of his fractured legacy and assemble them back together again.

None of Judge Derr's rulings in the Edwards case was a great surprise to Omaha defense lawyer Bill Gallup.

Judge Derr was known for almost always erring on the side of the prosecution, Gallup said.

Derr gave the defense side little wiggle room in criminal cases, Gallup said.

"As far as Judge Derr, you could never meet a nicer fellow," Gallup explained. "He came out of a silk-stocking civil law firm in Omaha with no experience in criminal cases. He's a strict law-and-order guy, a nice guy, a gentleman in the courtroom, but a pro-prosecution type of judge."

* * *

Tracey Ray, formerly of North Carolina, was hired to replace Kofoed and rebuild the lab's tarnished reputation. Originally from Massachusetts, Ray also had worked in Colorado and Kansas. Moving to Nebraska would not be an easy adjustment. Many of her holdover employees in the crime lab were Kofoed sympathizers, even after his career imploded.

On the other hand, she came on board at an opportune time. The sheriff still wanted to operate a state-of-the-art regional forensic laboratory.

Despite calls in the community to merge or shut down the county's crime lab, Sheriff Tim Dunning doubled down. He convinced his county board to spend more than $4 million in drug forfeiture funds to renovate the former Thomas Fitzgerald Veterans Home. In 2011, the new forensic services division on West Maple Road was unveiled to the media and public. The new county crime lab encompassed 10,000 square feet of space. The former facility Kofoed managed barely had 1,500 square feet.

The new crime lab was a breath of fresh air for the sheriff's department. It helped everyone forget about Kofoed's debacle and the wounds he caused.

As far as the Edwards murder case, Sheriff Dunning repeatedly assured reporters that Kofoed did not fabricate any blood against Edwards. But the case had not gone away. The new lawyer for Edwards had appealed to the Nebraska Supreme Court, requesting an evidentiary hearing surrounding the allegations of misconduct.

As Edwards's appeal process was heating up in the court system, a shocking diversion came out of nowhere at a wood trim and brick dwelling with a blue shed in the backyard.

It was the property of Bob Edwards, the father of Christopher Edwards.

After Kofoed went to prison for tampering with evidence in two prior murder cases, Douglas County District Judge J. Russell Derr was forced to decide whether to let Christopher Edwards' lawyers present evidence suggesting Kofoed also fabricated clues that were presented as exhibits during the historic 2007 jury trial held in Derr's courtroom.

Chapter 21

In early October of 2011, the Douglas County Sheriff's Office set foot on the property of Bob Edwards and his wife, Lynn, to dig for Jessica's skeletal remains.

According to the search warrant, authorities stated they were also looking for Jessica's pink shirt with a palm tree on the front, her blue jeans, purse, wallet, credit cards, and any type of identification. Her missing cellular phone, any weapons, or construction tools were also items of interest.

The dig for Jessica's bones at 1616 North 111th Street became a media spectacle. The deluge of press coverage made the community quickly forget about Kofoed's role in the original murder investigation, at least for the time being. This time, the CSI division, under its new leader Tracey Ray, was back at work, in the hunt for Jessica's skeleton.

A Bobcat dug up a portion of the backyard. More than five agonizing years had passed since Jessica's disappearance. Perhaps an end to this awful chapter in Omaha's history was about to be unearthed?

At the scene, Sheriff Dunning told the media that a Nebraska Wesleyan University archeologist's radar unit identified a large mass inside the concrete of Bob Edwards's patio. A cadaver dog also tracked a scent that something was buried in the ground. The sheriff previously received a handful of tips from people he did not want to identify, alerting him that the concrete patio was erected at the time of Jessica's slaying.

"Evidence and or her remains, we feel, are going to be found there," Sheriff Dunning asserted during an interview with Omaha's KETV.

The sheriff had badly misfired. Jessica's body was not buried on the property of Bob Edwards.

Two day of intense and suspenseful media coverage wound down with Sheriff Dunning waving the white flag. The sheriff acknowledged the large buried mass under Bob Edwards's patio was nothing more than a section of rock and concrete.

The stigma of the failed search for Jessica brought unflattering attention to the sheriff's office.

During the summer of 2012, the Douglas County Board approved a tort claim to pay Bob Edwards $5,064 to repair his damaged back yard.

"If Chris Edwards mans up and tells us where he put Jessica O'Grady, we would not be going through this," Dunning told the *Omaha World-Herald*. "It was a legitimate search that we had to do."

Brian Munnelly, the lawyer now trying to overturn their son's conviction, said the intent of the excavation by the sheriff's office was to cast suspicion on Bob Edwards. "They go in with such questionable probable cause based on some anonymous tip," Munnelly said. "It was a failed search, and nobody really knows why it happened."

* * *

That year, 2012, brought more unwelcomed attention to the Douglas County Sheriff's Office.

First, the Nebraska Supreme Court upheld Kofoed's felony tampering with evidence conviction out of Cass County.

Several weeks later, the Nebraska Supreme Court revisited the Christopher Edwards case. In a nutshell, Judge J. Russell Derr had concluded that even if Kofoed planted some evidence, the jury would have still found Edwards guilty anyway. The judge reasoned the bloody mattress clinched Edwards's guilt, and Edwards concealed other blood stains on the basement walls with shoe polish and white paint.

But the Nebraska Supreme Court had a strong differing viewpoint.

Its ruling remanded the Edwards case back to the Douglas County Courthouse, not for a new trial, but for a post-conviction evidentiary hearing.

Judge Derr was told by the state's supreme court that he erred in disallowing Edwards's new lawyers a chance to raise suspicions that Kofoed had planted false evidence to ensure their client's guilt.

The supreme court noted in its thirty-page ruling that Judge Derr applied the wrong legal standards in rejecting Edwards's due process claim.

"To the extent the court reasoned that Kofoed would not have fabricated evidence in Edwards's case because he had previously done so only when the State was desperate for evidence, we disagree," the state justices wrote. "Particularly in the 2003 investigation (of Ivan Henk) other evidence connected the suspect to the crime. The suspect confessed to the murder and led investigators to the place where he had disposed of the body. More important, the court incorrectly required Edwards to show that a jury would have acquitted him without the fabricated evidence. The court stated the issue as whether a jury would have found Edwards innocent but for Kofoed's alleged falsification of blood evidence found on the sword, the garden shears and the trunk gasket. It concluded that Edwards could not satisfy that standard. But this standard of materiality is incorrect."

The Edwards case marked the second high-profile murder in 2012 where Judge Derr had been overturned by the Nebraska Supreme Court. That same year, the state court ordered a new trial for Leroy Parmar Jr. He had been convicted years ago of first-degree murder and given a life sentence in the 1987 Ames Avenue apartment suffocation of Omaha resident Fred Cox, age 45. Parmar had always denied involvement in the slaying. In 2005, the Nebraska Commission on Public Advocacy asked Judge Derr to grant Parmar a new trial based on newly discovered DNA evidence. DNA samples excluded Parmar's DNA from approximately a half dozen different blood stains found on the murder victim's bedsheets. Yet Derr ruled the DNA evidence did not necessarily establish Parmar's innocence. Furthermore, the judge rejected Parmar's bid for a new trial, surmising that even if Parmar was granted a new trial, the verdict would not be any different.

"The State's conviction of Parmar depended heavily upon the testimony of two eyewitnesses, one of whom was an accomplice. And the state's theory of the crime, as presented through these eyewitnesses, was that only Parmar assaulted Cox and the only other participants in the crime were two women. (One woman) testified to seeing Parmar down by the top of Mr. Cox. But the post-conviction DNA testing results are clearly incompatible with the eyewitnesses' testimonies," the Nebraska Supreme Court stated.

In 2012, Parmar was freed from prison. He was not retried for the murder. However, the state supreme court's decision to overturn Judge Derr's initial denial of a new trial for Parmar attracted little attention around Omaha.

However, Judge Derr's handling of another post-conviction appeal, State vs. Christopher Edwards, was defining his career on the bench.

The Nebraska Supreme Court ruling issued on September 28, 2012, was a small victory for Edwards.

Begrudgingly, Judge Derr was forced to deal with the Edwards murder case, in essence, for a third time.

Munnelly, Edwards's new lawyer, was pleased with the Nebraska Supreme Court's ruling. He also gleaned that Judge Derr was not the most fair-minded judge at the Douglas County Courthouse—at least when it came to the murder case involving Chris Edwards.

By November 2012, Munnelly filed a legal brief asking Derr to recuse himself from further proceedings involving his client. "Edwards alleges that a reasonable person knowing the circumstances of this case would question the Court's impartiality under an objective standard of reasonableness," Munnelly wrote. "The defendant requests the Court to recuse itself from the case."

On Nov. 13, 2012, the judge who presided over Edwards's original trial and sentenced the defendant to one hundred years in prison did not offer any explanation for rejecting Munnelly's bid for a different judge.

Judge Derr wanted to remain in control of the Chris Edwards case. "Defendant's motion overruled," Derr wrote in his ruling.

Meanwhile, Edwards continued to serve his prison sentence at Nebraska's biggest maximum security prison, the Tecumseh State Correctional Institution.

As for Kofoed, the disgraced former Douglas County crime lab commander had packed his bags and left his hometown of Omaha after serving his prison sentence. During the latter part of 2012, he moved to North Carolina, to reunite with one of his brothers.

The painful mystery surrounding Jessica's hidden body continued.

Chapter 22

D.J. Ginsberg has poured his heart and soul into dozens of searches for Jessica's remains across Omaha's hilly terrain, waterways, and open fields.

He's founder of the United States ATV Search and Rescue unit in Omaha, a nonprofit group of volunteers affiliated with the Douglas County Sheriff's Office. Since 2006, his volunteer organization has dedicated thousands of hours trying to find the exact spot where Edwards hid Jessica's body. USATV has performed forty-seven search missions for Jessica. That's more than any other person they've tried to find.

"Even though I never met Jessica," Ginsberg said, "I feel like I know or knew her through her family. I've gotten close to the family. Jessica did not deserve that."

Ginsberg thinks Jessica's body was hidden within a five-mile radius of Edwards's aunt's home near 132nd and Blondo Streets in northwest Omaha.

Ginsberg called Edwards a "non-human animal." After all, Edwards has never confessed to the killing. He's never exhibited one ounce of remorse, either.

"Usually people like that eventually give it up," Ginsberg explained. "To continue to stay silent for years and years, the only reason he can be keeping this all to himself is that he's hiding something, and he's protecting somebody so that he's willing to take the fall, all on himself, because it will incriminate somebody else. I am not a police officer or a detective, but I think he did not act alone."

The team of dedicated searchers have pretty much eliminated two large bodies of water around Omaha, Cunningham Lake and Standing Bear Lake, Ginsberg conceded. However, back in 2006, searchers stumbled across a strange hole near Cunningham Lake where Edwards may have tried to bury Jessica, but quickly abandoned the site and put the body elsewhere, Ginsberg said.

Evidence was uncovered showing someone tried to dig a hole in the vicinity of Cunningham Lake. The hole was covered up with fresh dirt. "The digging was in a very woodsy area near a little stream," Ginsberg remembered. "We thought we were on to something there."

In 2006, Edwards stood about 5-foot, 7 inches and weighed 130 to 135 pounds, Ginsberg noted.

"At the time, this was a nineteen-year-old punk who only played golf, who didn't work out," Ginsberg explained. "To dig a six-foot-deep hole in the middle of the nighttime, he would never have been able to do that."

Wherever Edwards put Jessica's body, he probably got lucky, Ginsberg said.

"You have to remember, this punk was caught buying white-out paint to cover up the blood on his ceiling," Ginsberg said, "so this kid isn't very bright."

Ginsberg can't fathom how Edwards can live with himself, day after day, year after year, and continue to keep the circumstances of Jessica's murder and the disposal of her body a deep dark secret.

"People need closure," Ginsberg said. "I'm sure that it still hurts the family. All of us, we still talk about it. It will haunt all of us forever. I still believe [her body is] in the water somewhere."

* * *

By 2014, prosecutor Don Kleine was preparing to run for his third, four-year term in office. He had had a magnificent and exemplary record since winning office in 2006. Meanwhile, his lead prosecutor during the Edwards case, Leigh Ann Retelsdorf, was now a Douglas County District judge, just like Derr.

With Edwards's case being resurrected and back in the Nebraska legal spotlight, all eyes were squarely on Derr. Would the judge open the barn door? Would he conclude Kofoed's scandalous record at the crime lab also meant some of the evidence used against Edwards was poisonous fruit? Or would the judge be the gatekeeper? He could use his position and put to rest the embarrassing evidence-planting scandal that infected Omaha's law and justice system like a bad tumor.

It was hard to quantify the number of police officials, prosecutors, judges, and journalists who blindly put their faith in Kofoed over the years. One of those esteemed leaders happened to be Judge Derr. The sitting judge had no idea during the original Edwards proceedings that the CSI commander controlling all of the prosecution's evidence was an outright fraud. As a result, the pro-prosecution judge had allowed Kofoed's evidence and exhibits into Nebraska's first no-body murder trial conviction. Now, thanks to the Nebraska Supreme Court's intervention, Judge Derr was being forced to decide whether the original trial of Edwards was a sham.

* * *

March 13-14, 2014, marked an infamous milestone in the Edwards case.

An odd homecoming reunion of sorts was taking place on the fourth floor of the Douglas County Courthouse for key members of the original Edwards murder trial. Most of them preferred not to be in the courtroom—with a few notable exceptions including convicted killer Chris Edwards and his pair of tenacious lawyers, Brian Munnelly and Jerry Soucie. Soucie had worked as the public defender for Nick Sampson, one of the innocent men in Cass County who had been the victim of Kofoed's blood-planting scheme in the Murdock farmhouse killings.

For this grand occasion, a large throng of media returned for the extravaganza. Jessica's family, including her Aunt Shauna Stanzel, the family's media spokesperson, also attended.

The victim's family never fathomed Edwards might be on the verge of winning a major legal battle only seven years after a jury found him guilty of murdering Jessica.

By 2014, Edwards no longer looked like his old self. He had looked like a drummer in a 1990s grunge band. Now in his late twenties, Edwards had bulked up. He grew out long, wavy, brown hair that dangled down the middle of his back. He wore eyeglasses and sported large ugly tattoos along his right arm. These were not professional tattoos. You can only get these kinds of tattoos from a crude instrument wielded by another male prison inmate at the Tecumseh State prison where Edwards was housed.

The daylong courtroom spectacle also brought other infamous characters and fallen figures back to Omaha, such as Dave Kofoed, who was flown back to Omaha from North Carolina.

Later, Kofoed said he had no druthers about flying back to Omaha to testify against Chris Edwards. He wanted to assure everyone in the courtroom, including the judge, that all of the forensic clues used to convict Edwards were legitimate.

And, just like old times, when Kofoed walked into

the downtown Omaha courthouse, the television cameras all crowded around him. They followed the fallen crime lab commander as he walked down the marbled hallway, past the rotunda, and headed toward Judge Derr's fourth-floor courtroom.

Seven years had passed since the men last locked eyes on one another. At that time, Kofoed was a mighty law enforcement warrior. By 2014, crime had also uprooted and derailed Kofoed's life. He lost out on the privilege of leading the country crime lab to new heights at the modernized and expanded facility. After finishing prison, Kofoed escaped Omaha because he needed a fresh start far away from his hometown. Edwards was not so lucky. He ended up in Tecumseh, Nebraska, the state's most notorious maximum security prison, with beds for around a thousand hardened male prisoners consisting of drug dealers, killers, and predatory rapists.

When Kofoed took a bead on Edwards in court, he hardly recognized the killer.

"He may have been an attractive target at a facility like Tecumseh when he first arrived because of his age and really slight physique. He probably hooked up with someone just to survive. Bulking up and the tattoos had to be his way of coping and to fit in," Kofoed said.

Kofoed's testimony spanned both days. His star power was gone. His CSI superhero status had been reduced to a pile of ashes.

Edwards's lead lawyer Jerry Soucie saved his best

question for last. In the same Douglas County courtroom where Kofoed provided powerful testimony in 2007, Kofoed was forced to confront his own demons and professional failings.

"As a supervisor of the CSI unit back in 2006, at the time of the Edwards case, would you have assigned to one of your employees the task of collecting and processing evidence, transporting that evidence, if that individual had been convicted of fabricating evidence in another case?"

"No," Kofoed testified.

During the cross examination, Douglas County prosecutor Matt Kuhse tried to repair the tattered image of Kofoed, his office's former trusted confidant.

"Mr. Kofoed, I just have a couple of questions of you. When you were originally at the Edwards household on May 17, 2006, you went inside of the house?" Kuhse asked.

"Yes."

"And did that include the basement?"

"Yes."

"Inside the basement bedroom, you saw items of evidence regarding blood. You located some blood in there?"

"Yes."

"On a mattress?"

"Yes."

"On a headboard?"

"Yes."

"On a clock radio?"

"Yes."

"On the ceiling?"

"Yes."

"And on May 17, 2006, while you were inside the Edwards's basement bedroom, did you plant any of that evidence?"

"No."

"Did you plant the evidence on the mattress?"

"No."

"The headboard?"

"No."

"The clock radio?"

"No."

"The laundry basket?"

"No."

"The ceiling?"

"No."

"In fact, all of that blood was already there by the time you went into the residence because Omaha Police Department was there before you?"

"That's correct."

"That's all I have. Thank you, Mr. Kofoed," Kuhse concluded.

Interestingly, the prosecution chose to sidestep asking Kofoed about the ceremonial sword, the blood stains in the trunk or the hedge shears.

Judge Derr, tasked with being the courtroom gladiator for this most important of all clashes in the Edwards murder case, did not issue his ruling that day.

He would wait another ten months before issuing his momentous ruling.

As the courtroom soap opera played itself out, the media sought out Jessica's aunt for comment. She was asked about the prospect of another trial for Edwards.

"He's in a prison," Shauna Stanzel told Maggie O'Brien of the *Omaha World-Herald*. "And we're in a prison of our own not knowing where she's at. We deserve to know where she's at. He could do that anonymously. He doesn't have to do that publicly."

The post-conviction ruling was released on Jan. 15, 2015.

* * *

Back on May 16, 2006, when authorities invaded the downstairs bedroom, they noticed how Edwards's room was sweet smelling. The scented candles and plug-in air fresheners gave off a perfume-like aroma even though Jessica's blood soaked the bottom side of his mattress.

In many respects, Judge Derr's ruling carried that same savory smell of strawberries even though everyone realized Kofoed was a naughty skunk who had engaged in prior inexcusable evidence planting schemes using blood to further implicate the accused.

The ruling was carefully written.

Point by point, Judge Derr gave Kofoed the benefit of the doubt on all of the questionable evidence finds raised by the lawyers trying to win a new trial for Edwards.

"Kofoed stated he was in Defendant's residence on May 17, 2006 and observed blood on the mattress, headboard, ceiling and clock radio. He denies planting any of the blood evidence. He testified that all of the blood evidence was there when he arrived and that the Omaha Police Department was there when he arrived," Derr wrote.

"Before the State could knowingly use fabricated evidence, the evidence would have to be fabricated," Derr stated. "Therefore, the first question that must be addressed is, was it?"

The judge noted in his ruling that he was rejecting the notion that any blood in the trunk was planted by Kofoed.

"While Kofoed was at the residence at some point in the evening, there is no evidence that he had the ability to access the Accord and transfer blood evidence without observation by others."

The judge concluded that blood stains were in the trunk before the car was ever towed to Kofoed's crime lab. If the judge's ruling was accurate, that meant CSI Christine Gabig overlooked the blood stains while she inspected and photographed the wide-open trunk at the Edwards's home.

It also meant CSI Connelly also missed the blood stains the following day during his processing of the car that lasted almost six hours.

"Blood was found on the underside of the trunk directly below the stain on the trunk gasket," Derr concluded. "The stain on the trunk gasket is documented to be there while still in the Defendant's garage. That more blood was found on the underside of the trunk directly below the gasket stain is not unreasonable."

As for the murder weapon, the judge did not find any fault with the controversial sword that supposedly contained a pin drop of blood at the tip of the blade. "Defendant offered no evidence that the blood evidence on the sword was fabricated by Kofoed or anyone else," Derr wrote. "Any suggestion of fabrication of this evidence is purely guess, speculation and conjecture."

"There is little to no evidence that Kofoed fabricated evidence in this case," the judge went on to explain. "Defendant presented no evidence that controverted this testimony and there is no evidence in the entire record that establishes, much less even hints, that the State knowingly used false evidence to secure Defendant's conviction. For the foregoing reasons, Defendant's motion for post-conviction relief is denied."

Sheriff Dunning welcomed the judge's ruling. It was a huge blow to Edwards and his defense lawyers working feverishly on his behalf.

"Too many people saw that blood (of Jessica's) for the judge to believe anything else," Dunning noted. "I felt that the evidence in this case was so overwhelming that the judge would see that. If you take all of the evidence out of this case that would strictly pertain to Kofoed, we still have more than enough."

Sheriff Dunning also has reached his own conclusions regarding the controversy of his former crime lab commander tied to the Edwards case.

"I truly believe Kofoed did nothing wrong in this case. I know I was hoodwinked by him once before, but then so was a federal jury," Dunning said.

Moreover, the sheriff noted, the sword that contained the DNA of Jessica and her killer was retrieved by sheriff's deputy Tom Walter and the crime lab processing was handled by CSI Christine Gabig. "Kofoed had nothing to do with this key evidence," Dunning emphasized.

Those incriminating blood stains in the trunk of Edwards's trunk were actually found by CSI technician Bill Kaufhold, the sheriff said.

"Kofoed's only involvement here was photographing," Dunning said.

Two years removed from serving his prison sentence, David Kofoed returned to Omaha from North Carolina to testify at a post-conviction hearing for Edwards at the Douglas County Courthouse.

Douglas County Sheriff Tim Dunning made sure Omaha knew that his agency was in relentless pursuit of murder suspect Christopher Edwards and also investigating the possibility that her killer recruited someone else to help remove her body out of his bedroom.

Chapter 23

Although Derr's ruling let Edwards's conviction stand, hindsight is 20/20. Other people with intimate knowledge of the case question whether the scenarios presented during the murder trial were plausible.

"I think the blood on the sword and in the trunk was just the bow on the package for a case in which Edwards reasonably appeared to be guilty of killing his pregnant girlfriend," remarked Erin Sims, who runs the crime lab for the Lincoln Police Department, which is Nebraska's second largest city.

Sims, a certified crime scene investigator and bloodstain-pattern analyst in the International Association for Identification, had been asked to pinpoint precisely how much of Jessica's blood had saturated the mattress. According to Sims, most adult males have five to six liters of blood while females are closer to five liters. A two-liter blood loss leads to irreversible shock and death, unless immediate emergency responders arrive quickly to provide life-saving heroics, she explained.

Sims said the multitude of evidence at the crime scene proves that Jessica O'Grady met her demise in the Edwards residence. The defense's argument at the trial was not credible, she said.

"This was not a bloodstain associated with a common blood loss such as experienced by a menstrual cycle bloodstain or bloody nose," Sims explained. "The saturation stain would indicate that O'Grady's body was left on the mattress in a position long enough to bleed out, suggesting death.

"The mattress is the key piece of physical evidence that indicates Jessica O'Grady was killed at this location, by someone with access to the residence, with sufficient strength and time to clean up and dispose of her body," Sims continued. "And that motive and the most likely party of record is Chris Edwards."

A couple noteworthy clues used against Edwards bother Sims to this day.

She has a problem with the identification and portrayal by the Douglas County Sheriff's Office of the Bangkok battle sword as the murder weapon. Sims said she is pretty certain this was not the weapon used to kill Jessica.

"It is not appropriate to claim the sword as being the murder weapon when you do not have the victim's body in a condition suitable to examine wounds at autopsy and determine cause of death," Sims said. "The amount of blood located on the sword was alleged to be small and was not visible in the photos

I was shown."

The complete absence of visible blood stains upon the sword seems questionable, Sims pointed out. "Blood is difficult to clean up due to its adhesive nature," Sims said. "People try, but they often don't get it all. I would expect to see a great deal of blood on the sword if it were used to injure the victim. And depending on how it was cleaned, I would still expect to see significant blood in the crevices of the ornate features of the handle."

Sims pointed out the investigators never found the original bed sheets.

"One could theorize that since the body and bedding were disposed of, most likely the true murder weapon and anything else bloodstained, such as his own clothing, or items belonging to the victim were also disposed of," Sims explained. "The labeling of the sword as a murder weapon only served to up the wow factor of the case and check off the box for murder weapon recovery."

The blood stains of Jessica recovered in the trunk served a similar purpose.

The CSI photos of the interior trunk gave no impression Edwards left a bloody mess. There was no evidence showing Edwards tried to clean away the blood after the fact, but missed the stains on the interior lid, Sims said.

Sims said the bloodstain Kofoed recovered from the inside of the trunk lid appeared to be a transfer stain, diluted and about the size of a dime.

"It looked as if someone with diluted blood or who had re-hydrated dried blood with water had touched the ceiling of the trunk, possibly with the pad of a finger," she said. Sims said the blood stains looked like they were planted there after the fact.

"Finding the lone small stain in the trunk helped suggest that this was the vehicle used to dispose of the body. Check another box," she said.

"Blood is very hard to clean-up completely, especially on porous items like cloth and carpet. I would expect to see a lot more bloodstaining in the trunk or the removal of the (trunk) carpet if a body had been transported in this vehicle."

Sims views the sword as another dubious clue that emerged out of the Douglas County crime lab of Kofoed's during the build-up to Edwards's arrest.

"Had the sword been used, but not disposed of and kept as a souvenir (of the crime), I feel it is likely it would still contain a significant amount of blood on the ornate handle. If the sword had been used, I think they likely would have found gouge marks in the ceiling and in the wooden headboard of the bed given the overall length of the sword plus the assailant's arm, being swung in a position above the bed."

The bloodstain patterns indicate Jessica was beaten and stabbed, or stabbed multiple times, Sims pointed out. During one of the searches of the killer's bedroom, police confiscated a knife catalog that belonged to Edwards.

"The location of the stain on the mattress suggests head and or neck wounds," Sims said. "And I would have been looking for a smaller hand-held knife or axe-type weapon. I think due to the large amount of blood in the saturation stain, an artery was breached. No stains similar to an arterial spurt pattern were known to have been present at the scene, but we do know clean-up occurred."

* * *

Stuart James, the internationally known blood-stain analyst in Florida, said Kofoed's subsequent conviction for planting blood in two previous murder cases has made him rethink some aspects of the Edwards trial.

"I was shocked when I heard the allegations actually because my interactions with him were nothing but good. I never had any inkling," James said.

Nowadays, it's understandable why Kofoed has cast a cloud of suspicion upon himself related to the Edwards case.

The pruning shears that emerged out of the backseat of Edwards's car is one of the clues that has James scratching his head. That object had a tiny blood stain on a wooden handle but not on the blades. Based on the crime scene facts, the shears did not seem to have an obvious connection with the killing in the bedroom, James recalled.

"It is curious to me that her DNA was found on the hedge clippers, but nothing on the shovel," James said.

Based on his first-hand knowledge of the case, James said there was no reason for Kofoed to plant any blood against Edwards to ensure the suspect's guilt. "If he actually did that, it wasn't necessary," James said. "If that occurred, it was very stupid of him. She bled a lot. You could easily see where the basement ceiling had been painted over, especially the portions of the ceiling where there had been the cast-off blood stains."

Nowadays, James does not want to go on the record and say with confidence that the sword was used to kill Jessica, even though that was the evidence presented at the trial by the Douglas County prosecutors.

"I can't say," James conceded. "The only one who knows is Edwards."

Then again, Jessica's DNA was found on the tip of the blade and the black handle contained a mixture of DNA belonging to her and Edwards, James pointed out.

"That sword was kind of interesting. ... I can certainly see why that became an issue," James said.

He feels badly for Jessica's relatives. The courts may someday rule in favor of Edwards and grant him a new trial based on questions surrounding Kofoed's conduct.

"There was a lot of strong evidence there," James said. "Whether Edwards gets a new trial, that remains to be seen, I suppose."

* * *

Regardless of whether he crossed the line to ensure Edwards's guilt, Dave Kofoed's theory about Edwards's role in Jessica's murder should not be discounted by readers. Before he went to prison, Kofoed was an experienced and highly skilled CSI investigator. He had processed hundreds of crime scenes and homicides during his twenty-year career in police forensics.

Kofoed said he was not the least bit surprised Edwards chose to clam up and refused to tell the authorities what he did with Jessica's body.

"Over a period of time, I think it has become a power thing for him," Kofoed said. "He has one hold over Jessica's family. Obviously, he is a very selfish person. When I was incarcerated, I met a prisoner who knew Edwards from his time in Tecumseh. When we were alone in the laundry room, I asked him if Edwards ever told him what he did with Jessica. The guy would not answer me directly but implied that he had knowledge. I am not surprised (Edwards) never led authorities to the body."

Based on his relentless pursuit of justice for Jessica, Kofoed has his own theories about her untimely death. Kofoed suspects Jessica was struck multiple times on the bed of Edwards. Clearly, the attack was a surprise.

"She was either asleep or sitting on the bed," Kofoed predicted.

"He was in his basement," Kofoed said of Edwards. "His aunt and (her daughter) were apparently home in the far upstairs bedrooms the night Jessica went missing. I believe she was killed in the bedroom and never had a chance to defend herself. It was fairly quiet because she was blindsided. She never saw it coming."

Kofoed said he noticed Edwards had outdoor camping gear and packaging for sleeping bags in his bedroom, but no sleeping bags were there.

"I think Edwards placed her in a sleeping bag in his bedroom and pulled her body fully contained in the sleeping bag up the stairs from his bedroom into the garage and placed her in the trunk of his vehicle," Kofoed surmised. "There was a great deal of blood evidence in his bedroom but none on the carpeted steps leading out of the bedroom, or on the garage floor. The only blood evidence between the bedroom and vehicle was found on the upper trunk gasket."

Edwards lived in the vicinity of Omaha's Champions Run golf course area. The area was on the edge of Omaha's westward expansion near 132nd and West Maple Road. That busy intersection had a mix of retail and commercial developments including the Walgreens where Edwards bought the products to paint over sections of his blood spattered ceiling. Nearby, was an Applebee's, Target, McDonald's, and banks. A commercial strip mall on the other side of the street had a hodgepodge of small retail businesses and eateries including an Old Chicago's restaurant. Practically every business in that strip mall had its own garbage Dumpster out behind its back door in the alley way.

"My guess is that he placed her in a Dumpster near 132nd and Maple," Kofoed said.

Erin Sims runs the crime lab for the Lincoln Police Department, which is the second largest city in Nebraska. Sims suspects the blood stains identified in the trunk of Edwards' Honda were not legitimate.

Sims said that if Edwards killed Jessica with the battle sword later retrieved from his bedroom closet, there should have been gouge marks present on the headboard of his bed and marks on his ceiling.

Chapter 24

There are interesting parallels and hard lessons to take away from the crimes of Edwards and the evidence tampering conviction of commander Kofoed.

There were no eyewitnesses to either crime. The no-body murder trial of Edwards and the evidence tampering bench trial of Kofoed both rested on astoundingly strong circumstantial evidence.

Edwards chose not to testify in his defense at his 2007 jury trial. Kofoed chose not to take the stand to deny accusations during his 2010 bench trial.

Oakland, Nebraska, attorney Clarence Mock served as the legendary special prosecutor who secured Kofoed's stunning felony conviction. Ultimately, Mock chose not to present any evidence suggesting Kofoed fabricated bloody clues against Edwards.

Mock said his decision to punt on the Edwards case was mostly tactical trial strategy. Back in 2010, Mock was preparing for a jury trial in Cass County, a mostly farming region. The trial was not being held in metropolitan Omaha, where Kofoed was a popular figure at the Douglas County Courthouse amongst lawyers, judges, and fellow law enforcement officials.

Mock said he ultimately abandoned lumping in the Edwards murder case with the others for fear it might drag down the power and strength of his case against Kofoed. Instead, Mock focused on Kofoed's devious conduct in different Cass County murder cases. "I really thought his misconduct in the Murdock murders and Brendan Gonzalez case both had the same kind of Dave Kofoed saves the day," Mock said. "And both happened down there in Cass County."

Plus, Mock was preparing for a jury trial, not a bench trial, where he needed to convince all jurors of guilt; a deadlocked verdict was the essence of a failure.

Shockingly, just a couple of weeks before the start of the jury trial in Plattsmouth, Kofoed and his lawyer Steve Lefler waived Kofoed's right to a jury trial. They put the entire evidence planting case in the hands of veteran Cass County District Judge Randall Rehmeier, forcing him to be the lone arbiter of justice.

At the end of the trial, Mock was victorious. Kofoed headed to prison. Kofoed's role in saving the day during the build-up and media hype marching to the Edwards arrest and trial were never mentioned during the Cass County criminal trial.

"For persuasion purposes," Mock said, "I just

eliminated that. But with Kofoed coming in and finding the blood in the trunk of the car during a follow-up search that he called for, it had a lot of the same striking similarities of the Murdock case and it has the M.O. It's all Dave Kofoed coming in to make sure the people who look guilty stay guilty."

Kofoed's crimes blemished the state's otherwise squeaky clean reputation when it came to crime lab work and criminal forensics.

"It is difficult to truly know what was going on in Kofoed's mind," Sims said. "I don't think David Kofoed thought he could ever get caught. I think he was careful. I think he thought he was smart. I think he thought he was helping to convict the right person or persons who might otherwise get off on a technicality. I think he managed what individuals in his lab knew and worked on."

One of Kofoed's former CSIs now works with Sims at the Lincoln Police Department. "One of his previous employees told me that sometimes Kofoed would ask them to change the wording in reports," Sims revealed. "The employee told me they never knew why it was important to make the change, but they followed orders thinking as the boss, Kofoed must be correct. The employee said it was common to only work a small portion of a case and not know what was going on with the rest of it."

Kofoed benefitted from his hometown police department's buddy system and good ole' boy network. Sims noted that Kofoed's late father was a former Omaha Police Department sergeant. "I am betting that filling out the job application form was merely a formality. When Sheriff Dunning offered Kofoed a job, that also was likely merely a formality," she said. "I think these hiring practices make it easy for someone like Kofoed to slip into a CSI job. I also think Kofoed became accepted as one of the law enforcement officer family without having to pass all of the tests and jump all of the hurdles. I think those around him trusted him blindly and without reserve. Looking back, we should not be surprised this happened and continues to happen around the country."

In all likelihood, Kofoed gave little thought to the possibility that his evidence planting stunts would lead to the reversal of any legitimate convictions against real criminals, Sims said. "The reputation that Kofoed was building for himself as the best of the best was just strengthened by these minor additions and in his mind, he was not hurting anyone. I think he thought this was a win/win."

Darnel Kush, the former Douglas County crime lab technician who helped the FBI take down her boss, also suspects the blood in the trunk was manufactured by her former supervisor. "If Kofoed did not plant evidence in the Edwards case, then yes, that would have been his finest hour, unfortunately, that was not the case," Kush said, "too many similarities with the Edwards case and other cases. Kofoed was becoming better at planting the evidence and his integrity was becoming less. His motivation was to be the best crime scene investigator and at this time, he had everyone fooled."

Still, Kush said she does not want readers to think Edwards was innocent.

"The evidence is pretty overwhelming as far as Jessica dying in that room of Edwards," she said. "I think he's guilty, but I don't think that Edwards got a fair trial."

Like Edwards, Kofoed has never accepted responsibility nor acknowledged guilt for his crimes. He did not apologize to Matt Livers or Nick Sampson for planting blood against them in 2006, even though they were both proven to be innocent of killing farmers Wayne and Sharmon Stock.

Rather, Kofoed has maintained in numerous media interviews that he, too, was innocent and that he has never planted evidence in a single criminal case.

He still wants people to believe that.

"What happened should never have happened," Kofoed said. "It was wrong and there is no way that the true story will ever be told. I wish it would be for my daughter, my mother and my brothers, and for the CSI team I once worked with.

"I pissed off the wrong folks. I guess what amazes me most is that we won a federal jury trial after about forty minutes of actual deliberation."

In 2014, a federal judge in Omaha issued a civil judgment of $6.5 million against Kofoed for planting blood evidence against Livers and Nick Sampson, thus keeping them incarcerated for a double murder they did not commit. Their civil lawyers consider the judgment largely symbolic. Because Kofoed maintains he is broke, the lawyers don't expect to collect on the judgment against him.

* * *

Whether Edwards will get another day in court remains to be seen. Clearly, Judge Derr's denial of a new trial was a major blow to his defense lawyers, Jerry Soucie and Brian Munnelly. They put forth an all-out effort to win their convicted murderer another trial. Derr's ruling was a huge defeat for them. But they are not finished.

They are now headed back before the Nebraska Supreme Court with their appeal. Soucie, one of Nebraska's most seasoned criminal defense trial lawyers, said the tainted evidence schemes of Kofoed were not always the same or about bringing more notoriety to himself.

Soucie points to the recovery of the battle sword from Edwards's closet and the tiny speck of blood later found on the tip by CSI Christine Gabig. She was Kofoed's most trusted confidant at the crime lab, Soucie explained.

"Kofoed said it best. He was in charge and could assign someone else to find the planted evidence; brilliant plan," Soucie said, recalling a lawsuit deposition Kofoed once gave.

"The sword was in his custody," Soucie continued. "Gabig was his star pupil. She really hadn't 'found' anything up to that point to give her a bone to make her happy and get to testify. Edwards was THE big case for the Douglas County Sheriff's Office at the time. They were the lead agency and CSI had a blank check."

* * *

On the other side of the aisle, the Edwards case has been dogged for years by rumors that somebody must have helped the killer remove Jessica's body from his home.

Dunning said he remains suspicious of the killer's dad. He thinks Bob Edwards knows more about Jessica's homicide than what authorities can prove in a court of law.

Back in 2006, Douglas County had Bob Edwards furnish a DNA sample to compare against the crime scene clues. Authorities never found any physical evidence to link Bob Edwards to the murder, and he has never been charged with any crime. Omaha journalists who covered his son's jury trial portrayed Bob Edwards as combative. One story mentioned how he shoved a television cameraman while inside the Douglas County Courthouse.

When asked if Bob Edwards cooperated during the sheriff's office investigation, Dunning remarked, "He did only what he had to do."

"I have always suspected Bob's involvement,"

Dunning added. "The evidence in this case was overwhelming against Chris, over two hundred-plus items. Why wouldn't he want to give some fatherly advice and ask that his son give the O'Grady family some closure? Why was he so concerned about the relationship with the girlfriend, Michelle Wilken? Was he concerned that Chris might confide in her? Why was Bob so concerned about what Chris might say on the phone from the Douglas County Jail? Would Chris implicate him in some way?"

Dunning said he watched Bob Edwards's demeanor after the sheriff's office arrived at his Omaha home to dig up his backyard patio in October of 2011 during the unsuccessful two-day attempt to find Jessica's bones on the property.

"We handed him the search warrant, and he said nothing but went to his neighbors' yard and watched," Dunning remembered. "If this happened to me, and I was innocent, you would have to chain me to a tree to control my outrage."

Lefler, the original defense lawyer, said there was absolutely no chance possible that Chris Edwards's father Bob Edwards was involved.

"I'm not even granting you that Chris killed her," Lefler said. "But my understanding is that Bob Edwards was in Chicago or some other city far away where it would have been impossible to make the drive. That theory was floated before the trial started. If they had developed any evidence that Bob was involved, if the state had developed any evidence that someone assisted Chris in disposing the body, I guarantee you someone would have been charged back then."

Sheriff Dunning corroborated Lefler's statement that Bob Edwards was in Chicago at the time of Jessica's slaying in Omaha.

Actually, in the vast majority of no-body murders, the killer acted alone when disposing of the body, noted DiBiase, the nationally recognized expert researcher on no-body murders. That kind of statistical data helps debunk the rampant speculation that Christopher Edwards had to have help in getting rid of Jessica.

"In almost all cases, they are not going to give up control by having somebody else there who knows about it," DiBiase explained.

Given that scenario, readers should not anticipate that Jessica's murderer will make a full confession of guilt and reveal where he put her body.

"My guess is that Edwards has convinced himself that he didn't do it," suggested Omaha journalist Tom Becka. "Or maybe his father convinced him he didn't do it, so why would he admit where the body was?

"If he was ever going to tell what he did with the body, he would have done it prior to conviction, so he could have worked out a deal with the prosecutor. There is no gain in him leading authorities to the body now."

Sheriff Dunning, the key law enforcement official who spearheaded the case, also tends to doubt Edwards will have a change of heart in the near future.

"Chris Edwards is very close to whomever assisted him in the body removal and disposal. Unless he gets mad at the person, there is no incentive for him to reveal this secret," Dunning said.

Dunning said his investigators have ruled out Michelle Wilken, the mother of Edwards's daughter, as an accomplice. She was not involved in the removal of Jessica's body or transporting Jessica's car to the parking lot near the ShopKo Plaza near 144th and West Center Road, Dunning said.

"Michelle was cooperative but clueless about this crime and not suspected in any part of the homicide, disposal of body, or cleanup of the scene," Dunning explained.

The sheriff contends the killing was premeditated, and the computer forensics work performed by his investigators proved that during the trial.

"Chris Edwards was researching the anatomy of the human body on his computer," Dunning said. "This would specify which veins would produce quick injury and death."

Moreover, the motive for murder was straightforward in the eyes of the sheriff.

"I believe he had the inability to handle the fact that

he now had two pregnant girlfriends," Dunning said of Edwards. "I believe he saw this pregnancy as a threat to his relationship with Wilken."

Dunning wants to help Jessica's family heal, but knows that will never happen unless Edwards confesses to the killing and reveals where he concealed her corpse.

"I think what bothers us even more is not knowing who assisted in the disposal of Jessica's body," Dunning pointed out. "No one can possibly believe that 125-pound (sic) Chris Edwards picked up 135-pound Jessica O'Grady, dead weight no less, and carried her from the residence by himself. There were no drag marks on the floor. Someone helped carry her out of there and into the trunk of his car."

Epilogue

Since December 2012, I've worked as an investigative journalist for Wisconsin's largest news operation, Gannett Wisconsin Media, based in Appleton, Wisconsin. Prior to that, I was a reporter for nine years at the *Omaha World-Herald* newspaper. I worked there when the Jessica O'Grady coverage unfolded. However, I was not involved with the initial coverage. My colleagues did solid and meaningful reporting on her case. I was in the midst of full-blown reporting on the senseless shotgun slayings of Nebraska farmers Wayne and Sharmon Stock.

Just three weeks before Jessica's case touched a nerve, the Stocks, a beloved farm couple in their fifties, were slain in their upstairs bedroom on Easter Sunday night, about sixty miles from Omaha. Through my stories chronicling their horrific murders, I came to know Douglas County CSI commander Dave Kofoed. I interviewed Kofoed numerous times over the course of several years. Some of our interviews took place at his sheriff's office in northwest Omaha.

Later, they took place at the minimum-security prison in Lincoln, where he served out his sentence for felony evidence tampering. Kofoed's fall from grace resulted in my first book, *Bloody Lies: A CSI Scandal in the Heartland*, published in June 2014 by The Kent State University Press in Ohio.

During my research for *Bloody Lies*, I never lost sight of the fact that Kofoed became the main law enforcement hero of the Chris Edwards murder case. And, I also realized how Jessica O'Grady's murder happened AFTER Kofoed planted blood in two other unrelated high-profile murder cases that were solved under his watch.

I began to review as many Douglas County CSI reports that I could get my hands on. My goal was simple: sort out fact from fiction, and find aspects of the Jessica O'Grady homicide investigation that were overlooked. Although I was not present during the original jury trial proceedings in the Douglas County Courthouse of Judge Derr against Edwards, in many respects, my outside perspective put me in a better position to give the case a fresh set of eyes after the fact. By 2012, I had covered an Edwards hearing before the Nebraska Supreme Court for my former Omaha newspaper.

From my perspective, aside from the bloody mattress, the case was dominated by a number of highly unusual clues that emerged under Kofoed's watch.

To this day, Nebraskans vividly recall the Jessica O'Grady murder case because of the Bangkok battle sword. And yet the sword may have been nothing more than a smokescreen, a false piece of evidence orchestrated to secure Edwards's arrest and subsequent conviction.

James Martin Davis, the first criminal defense lawyer for Chris Edwards, said he doubts the sword was the real murder weapon. "I think it was a knife," Davis told me confidently, during our interview on June 23, 2015.

At this point, however, the allegations of tainted evidence are just allegations against a disgraced former crime lab director. David Kofoed was never charged with a crime surrounding the Edwards case. As for Kofoed, he insists he did not manufacture any clues against Edwards.

"I want you to know from me directly that I did not plant evidence," Kofoed told me in June 2015.

Davis said the evidence against Chris Edwards was pretty substantial, regardless of any misdeeds involving Kofoed. "Kofoed did not soak that mattress in blood," Davis told me. "And he did not splash the blood marks all over the wall."

On the flip side, the sheriff's office belief that Chris Edwards had an accomplice help dispose of the body remains unsubstantiated.

Some investigators surmised Edwards either had help moving Jessica's car to the shopping plaza or someone gave him a ride home after abandoning it there.

It's my belief Chris Edwards did not use his own car to remove Jessica's body on the night of her murder. I think it's more likely he used her car.

However, the Douglas County CSI unit did not seriously investigate that scenario back in 2006, leading up to the arrest of Edwards.

For starters, Kofoed did not have immediate access to Jessica's vehicle. Therefore, he had no opportunity to plant blood in her car. Since her car was found at an Omaha city shopping mall, it was impounded at the Omaha Police Department's secured facility. Secondly, Kofoed identified the blood stains in Edwards's car barely twenty-four hours after his agency retrieved the bloody mattress.

Therefore, in many ways, Jessica's car became an afterthought in the case. And yet DNA tests performed at the University of Nebraska Medical Center during the summer of 2006 determined that a partial profile containing Chris Edwards's DNA was discovered on the driver's side door of Jessica's Hyundai. A full DNA profile of Jessica was obtained from her driver's side door. The Omaha police's crime lab found a handful of unknown latent fingerprints within Jessica's car, but nothing of any consequence in the trunk of Jessica's car. The shopping plaza where her car was recovered did not contain any video surveillance cameras.

However, if Edwards got rid of the body on the night of her killing, it makes far more sense to use her car, not his car. Why would Edwards take the risk of placing any blood, DNA, or trace evidence into his car? To use his own car means that Edwards had to lift Jessica's slain body into his Honda Accord car, seek out a safe disposal site in the middle of night. After hiding her body, he still had to return home, park, then get into Jessica's car, drive it to the shopping center five miles away, park her car, dispose of her keys, and walk all the way home under the cloak of darkness.

Sims, the crime lab director at the Lincoln, Nebraska Police Department, said she suspects Chris Edwards used Jessica O'Grady's car on the night of the killing.

"I agree with your theory," Sims told me.

"The easiest and fastest way to accomplish this would be to load everything into the victim's car and find a disposal site or sites for the body and other moveable objects. If you do this alone, you still need the car to get back close to home. I'd probably make a trip through a carwash, wipe it down, and park it somewhere that the victim herself might have parked it. I'd walk home from there and when I got home, try to clean up. I'm sure he knew he should get rid of the mattress, but given its size, and the difficulty of getting it out of the basement by himself, he chose to flip it and hope for the best. I don't think anyone helped him with the disposal, or they would have surely helped with the mattress as well. It also makes little sense to load a bloody body into your own car, when you need to get rid of the victim's car as well."

So, was all the forensic evidence used in State vs

Edwards real? Was any evidence tainted?

Chris Edwards knows the truth, and he still isn't saying a word to anyone, not even to me.

The vast majority of people in Omaha—including the O'Grady family—are vehemently opposed to the courts granting a second trial for Edwards. I can understand their point. I can't emphasize enough for readers that Chris Edwards is not someone who happens to be innocent. You don't see the nationally acclaimed Innocence Project fighting on his behalf. In fact he's one of the worst kinds of killers because he's managed to punish the O'Grady family through his intentional silence.

At the time of this book's publication, the Nebraska Supreme Court was in the early stages of reviewing the Edwards post-conviction appeal. His lawyers, Soucie of Lincoln and Munnelly of Omaha, say they expect the Nebraska Supreme Court to hold oral arguments during the fall months of 2015. A ruling from the state supreme court isn't anticipated until 2016.

I estimate Edwards's odds at winning a new trial at far less than 50 percent. However, it would not be a stretch for Nebraska's justices to decide a new trial is warranted, given the court's familiarity with Kofoed's evidence fabricating crimes in other Nebraska murder cases the state supreme court has scrutinized.

We'll see what the next year brings. The ruling by the Nebraska Supreme Court will be monumental, whichever way the court decides.

* * *

As of July 2015, Edwards has kept quiet for more than nine years about Jessica's murder and the whereabouts of her body.

He refused to testify at trial. He refused to make a statement at sentencing, instead letting his overbearing father Bob Edwards address the court as his proxy. He has rebuffed all news media interview requests over the years. He chose to ignore my request to interview him about Jessica's murder for this book.

In June of 2015, I asked Chayse Bates, Jessica's former long-time boyfriend, what he would ask Chris Edwards, if ever given an opportunity to have a face-to-face conversation with the convicted killer.

"I would ask him to reveal what he did with her body, so she can have a proper burial for everyone to say goodbye," Bates told me. "And I would ask him why he did it? What would possess you to harm a smart and beautiful girl?"

So why has Chris Edwards chosen to stay silent all this time?

If Jessica's lover committed the beastly crime alone, then why reject the plea bargains? Manslaughter carried a twenty-year maximum. And with good time credit, Edwards was assured of serving a maximum of ten years, perhaps far less. Bottom line, he would be freed before his thirtieth birthday.

At this point, he won't be released from prison until he's in his late sixties, if he survives that long at Tecumseh.

Surely, he knew his menstrual blood defense theory would anger the jury. And yet he balked at the plea deal anyway. Why? Could Edwards be protecting someone? Could he be willing to take the fall for the murder all by lonesome himself?

Edwards must have a motive to keep his mouth shut all this time, even as he has adjusted to his miserable and lowly life at Nebraska's most dangerous maximum security prison.

Tecumseh will never be confused with the Arizona Biltmore Hotel in Phoenix. Tecumseh is where the state of Nebraska's worst and notorious murderers, violent rapists, and pedophiles are sent to whittle away their time and eventually die. In May 2015, the prison had a horrific riot. These inmates caused at least $500,000 in damage, and the prisoners killed two pedophile inmates during the rioting. It's crazy to fathom that Edwards has resigned himself to wasting the rest of his natural life being housed there.

"Everything is for sale in prison. People hustle everything, including their dignity, it just depends on what you're willing to pay for that service and item," remarked Kelly Asmussen, a professor of criminal justice at Peru State University in far southeastern Nebraska. He had worked for fourteen years at the Nebraska State Penitentiary in Lincoln and now teaches a college course at the Tecumseh prison open to inmates who are interested in changing their ways, including convicted killers. Edwards has not tried to enroll in his class, Asmussen said.

From Asmussen's vantage point, Chris Edwards's bulked up physique, his long wavy hair, and the crude prison tattoos show Edwards has decided to assimilate within the prison. He wants to fit in and be known as a rebel, a killer who despises the prison authority."I can't imagine being a college-aged student accused and found guilty of murder and going to prison at twenty years old and knowing this is where you're housed at. I can't imagine it," Asmussen said of Edwards.

But Edwards can turn his life around if he seeks forgiveness, Asmussen said. But first, Jessica's killer needs to reach that moment of deep despair. The turning point for most inmates at Tecumseh comes when they look themselves in the mirror. Who do they see in the reflection? Are they willing to seek forgiveness?

Unless Edwards decides to seek forgiveness, Jessica O'Grady's family and friends will remain condemned to a life of hell, Asmussen said. For them, there will always be constant reminders of her disappearance and murder. They will be shackled by a stream of endless questions, all because Edwards has not sought forgiveness.

"The family, because they have not found her, they have a hole in their heart, a huge hole in their heart,"

Asmussen said. "They are victimized annually. They are reliving that trauma every time there's a birthday, the anniversary of the murder, or the trial, all of that. Her parents and her family are, in reality, victims every day and it kills them and makes their quality of life an open sore, and it never gets healed."

At the time of this book, Edwards was nearing his twenty-ninth birthday. The little girl who was conceived by Chris Edwards and Michelle Wilken back in December of 2005 is now in grade school, almost nine years old. She is growing up fast.

One person I interviewed for this book said Michelle has started dating someone else, and she only visits Edwards in prison on occasion. Like Edwards, Michelle did not respond to my personal request for an interview as I finished writing this book.

* * *

Chris, if by chance you read this book, it's time for you to think of your own daughter, Macy.

How would you react if someone terrorized her like the pain you brought to everyone touched by Jessica's savage murder upon your bed? True, what's done cannot be undone. You cannot bring Jessica back. At the time of Jessica's murder, you carried a Bible in the backpack of your car, the CSI reports show. It's time for you to seek redemption and forgiveness. You can still salvage the rest of your life by helping the others heal. Help Jessica's survivors be whole.

Here's my suggestion: contact your warden or one

of your prison ministry staff. Put a proposal in writing that you're willing to reveal the true facts and circumstances of Jessica's homicide. Stop acting like a cowardly killer. Identify the spot of Jessica's hidden body or cough up the names of those who do know.

Put in writing that you'll plead guilty to felony manslaughter and that you are willing to serve out an entire twenty-year prison sentence. In essence, with credit for your prior time served, you would remain a state of Nebraska inmate until the summer of 2026. You would get out of Tecumseh at age 39, that's still plenty of time for you to regain your freedom, reunite with your growing daughter and become a productive person. I don't think my proposal is out of line. It brings Jessica's family some comfort and closure in recovering her remains and moving on in the grieving process. Bottom line, your life needs to be focused on seeking their forgiveness, not on getting more prison tattoos with daggers, skulls, or crossbones across your hairy arms.

If I were you, I would not hold out hope the Nebraska Supreme Court will overturn your second-degree murder conviction. Earlier this year, the same court rejected an appeal from a different Nebraska killer, Richard Cook. Cook also tried to use Kofoed as a scapegoat for his first-degree murder conviction, but Cook's appeal didn't stand the light of day.

So I say, please give Jessica O'Grady's loved ones their daughter back. Allow Jessica a proper and fitting cemetery burial with flowers, a tombstone, and eternal rest. For no other reason, do this for the sake of your daughter, Macy.

Let her see through your own life that people who are prone to tremendous evil don't always have to stay evil forever.

There is still time on earth to change your wicked ways; you're not even thirty. But the time to act is urgent. It's now.

Jessica O'Grady's car was first impounded by the Omaha Police Department, not the Douglas County Sheriff's Office crime lab. Based on a variety of factors, Kofoed was not able to give serious consideration to the scenario that Christopher Edwards disposed of his dead girlfriend's body in her vehicle, not his car.

*Since June of 2007, Christopher Edwards has remained a
prisoner at the Tecumseh State Correctional Institution in
rural southeastern Nebraska. This prison houses Nebraska's
most notorious and hardened killers and criminals. Edwards
was 20 when he started serving his 100-year sentence. In
October of 2015, he turns 29.*

Thank you for reading Body of Proof. I hope you enjoyed it as much as I enjoyed writing it. If you did like it then I'd appreciate it if you provided an honest review at http://wildbluepress.com/BodyofProofReviews.

You can sign up for advance notice of new releases at: http://wildbluepress.com/AdvanceNotice

Thank you for your interest in my books,

John Ferak

Now For The First Time
As An eBook and Audio Book!

NO STONE UNTURNED: The True Story Of The World's Premiere Forensics Investigators

"A fascinating journey into the trenches of crime [investigation]"
--Lowell Cauffiel, New York Times bestselling author of House of Secrets

Order Your Updated Copy of NO STONE UNTURNED at

wildbluepress.com/ NSU-BM

NO STONE UNTURNED recreates the genesis of NecroSearch International as a small eclectic group of scientists and law enforcement officer who volunteer their services to help locate the clandestine graves of murder victims and recover the remains and evidence to assist with the apprehension and conviction of the killers. Known early on as "The Pig People" because of their experiments in locating graves using the carcasses of pigs (because of their similarities to human bodies), NecroSearch has evolved and expanded into one of the most respected forensic investigation teams in the world. In NO STONE UNTURNED, New York Times bestselling author Steve Jackson, the author of **BOGEYMAN** and MONSTER, vividly tells the story of this incredible group and recounts some of their most memorable early cases that if taken separately would each make great true crime books.

See the Next Page for More about No Stone Unturned

"The book covers the group's quirky beginnings and digs into its most important cases suspensefully; Jackson's sharp eye misses nothing in the painstakingly rendered details. A must-have for true crime fans, it should also be of great interest to anyone fascinated with the practical applications of science."
—Publisher's Weekly (Starred Review)

"A fascinating account of a group of extraordinary people who volunteer their time and expertise to locate hidden murder victims for the police and prosecutors. ... Recommended for public and academic libraries."
—Library Journal

"No Stone Unturned" delves into cases that would make good novels, but they're real. Furthermore, he describes a group of uncommon people performing uncommon tasks, and he does it with respect, accuracy and genuine style."
—Ron Franscell, bestselling author of The Darkest Night.

Order Your Updated Copy
of NO STONE UNTURNED at
wildbluepress.com/NSU-BM

Check out more True CRIME and Crime Fiction from WildBlue Press

www.WildBluePress.com

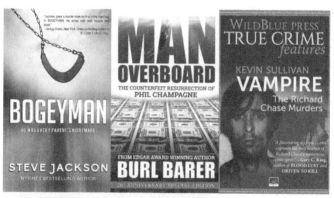

Go to WildBluePress.com to sign
up for our newsletter!

By subscribing to our newsletter you'll
get *advance notice* of all new releases as well
as notifications of all special offers. And you'll
be registered for our monthly chance to win
a **FREE collection of our eBooks and/or audio
books** to some lucky fan who has posted an
honest review of our one of our books/eBooks/
audio books on Amazon, Itunes and GoodReads.

Made in the
USA
Middletown, DE